END of the LINE

END of the LINE
Quitting Cocaine

Kathleen R. O'Connell

The Westminster Press
Philadelphia

Book design by Gene Harris

First edition

Published by The Westminster Press®
Philadelphia, Pennsylvania

PRINTED IN THE UNITED STATES OF AMERICA

9 8 7 6 5 4 3 2 1

Library of Congress Cataloging in Publication Data

O'Connell, Kathleen R.
　End of the line.

　Bibliography: p.
　1. Cocaine habit—Treatment. I. Title.
RC568.C6O36 1985　　616.86′3　　85-7135
ISBN 0-664-24669-9 (pbk.)

To my father,
William Edward O'Connell,
and to the interest in
and love for
clinical work and pharmacology
that he passed on to me

This is the true joy in life, the being used for a purpose recognized by yourself as a mighty one . . . the being a force of Nature instead of a feverish selfish little clod of ailments and grievances complaining that the world will not devote itself to making you happy.

> —George Bernard Shaw,
> dedication to *Man and Superman*

Contents

Acknowledgments

First comes the work of Dr. Maria Fagnan, editor and researcher, whose talent and caring made this book possible. I thank her for her contribution. I also wish to thank Carol Fairhurst, who typed the manuscript.

Next are the patients I have treated for cocaine addiction, especially those who contributed their case histories, their stories, their poems, and their letters. Their interest in helping others is what this book is all about.

And I would like to acknowledge the work of John Lofft, M.D., at the Washington Hospital Center, where I received much of my training in the early 1970s, and of Milton Erickson, M.D., to whom I owe so much in the area of treatment methodologies.

I would also like to mention the staff at Star Lodge Hospital and The Camp, who are so supportive in working with patients.

But most of all I would like to acknowledge all those who are able to receive help, now that we understand that cocaine is an addictive drug, and to remember all those who lost their lives because of their cocaine addiction and our lack of knowledge. I hope these seemingly unnecessary deaths will be reduced in the future as a result of our understanding of cocaine addiction as a treatable illness.

There was no reason to eat or sleep anymore. Cocaine was better than eating, better than sleeping. Cocaine was living curled in a cloud's diaphanous white side. Cocaine was wearing the sky for eyes.

—Kate Braverman,
Lithium for Medea

Introduction

I am writing this book because too many people are dying from cocaine addiction, and because in my work I see too many people who are suffering disabilities, including brain hemorrhages and strokes, as a result of their cocaine use. I say "too many people," because both the general public and the medical community are about fifteen years behind the times in their knowledge of cocaine addiction. Our understanding of alcoholism is more realistic now because of public and media education; most people today know that alcoholism is a treatable illness. They do not yet understand that cocaine addiction is treatable as well.

Experts disagree on definitions of addiction, and it is true that cocaine withdrawal does not produce symptoms like the extremes of heroin withdrawal or the delirium tremens of alcoholism. But this doesn't mean that cocaine isn't addicting. Joel Fort, in *The Addicted Society,* describes the drug abuser as "a person whose use is so heavy that it measurably damages health, job or school, and/or social functioning." And Dr. Richard Miller, founder of Cokenders, says in a 1984 audio-tape lecture that

the public has been misled into believing that there is a critical difference between physical and psychological reactions to cocaine. People believe cocaine to be safe just because they have heard it is not physically addicting. That is, it does not cause physical withdrawal symptoms like heroin. But try to tell a person who is abusing himself with cocaine that it is all in his mind. Is it possible to have a mind without a body, or a body without a mind? Can you minimize your discomfort by telling yourself it is all in your mind? Of course not. The fact is, if you can't quit, you are hooked! And being hooked on cocaine invariably leads to health problems or impaired economic or social functioning, all of which are very serious conditions. My operating definition of addiction is an uncontrollable urge.

The average users—and abusers—of cocaine are ordinary people, like the ones you work with, play with, and live with. Dr. Mark Gold, who established the 800-COCAINE hotline, notes that they are usually "men and women who are on their way up and who, by most yardsticks used to measure success, are successful" (*800-COCAINE,* p. 1). They didn't start out to be cocaine addicts, they began by experimenting with the drug at a party or as part of their relationship with a friend, lover, or spouse. And most people who begin this way don't become addicts. The problem is that it is impossible to predict which individuals will find cocaine a high-risk drug. For them, cocaine may be the first psychoactive drug they have tried, or it may be only the most recent in a series going back to adolescent experimentations with alcohol, marijuana, and whatever else they could find in the family medicine chest. For those who do become addicted, Dr. Gold says (p. 12),

> the description of cocaine as a "recreational" or "social" drug is a sick joke. Recreation does not usually take over one's entire life and destroy it. The loneliness of the cocaine abuser makes the view that coke is a social drug a lie. By their own account, use of the drug has cut them off, set them adrift from most of their previously meaningful relationships.

Cocaine has made a permanent change in their lives. The cocaine addict can never go back to what he or she was before.

Of course, it's not only cocaine that can become addicting. Food, sex, chocolate, gambling, even work can be overdone to the point of addiction. Cocaine is a more serious problem just because it causes loss of control in individuals who would seem to be otherwise in charge of their lives. The recovering cocaine addict must be careful not to become addicted to something else in the course of the recovery, and this is why a program of continuing therapy and support is so important. The cocaine addict must learn a more realistic understanding of life, the good times and the bad, and this is why I say that addiction can be the greatest gift the addict has ever received.

It's easy to get a very different view from the media, where the preoccupation with cocaine abuse by famous personalities has been sensational. We all know that cocaine is a glamorous drug and that it is expensive. We need to learn that it is also dangerous. Smoking cocaine is a fire hazard, if nothing else, and injecting cocaine with dirty needles can cause infections and disease. Even snorting cocaine is dangerous, contrary to popular opinion; many users now have chronic nasal and sinus conditions that cannot be cured. And however cocaine is used, it can certainly aggravate such known or unknown physiological conditions as heart problems, high blood pressure, and epilepsy. Cocaine use, even in relatively small quantities, can indeed be the critical factor in an attack or seizure that results in death.

The message we need to hear now, as a society, is that cocaine addiction is an illness and that it is treatable. Much of what we have learned in the past fifteen or twenty years in treating alcoholism and other drug addictions can be used in helping people addicted to cocaine.

Over the past twelve years I have treated approximately 2,000 people recovering from cocaine addiction, and I have talked to many others. In addition, I lived through the drug culture of the 1960s myself, in New York. I often think back to that time and to the young people, ages 17, 18, and 19 then, who are not alive today. Their use of drugs and their violent life-style were responsible for their deaths. I am glad that there are many more resources available now to help people who have problems with drug abuse.

This book is intended to emphasize ways of helping people who have problems with cocaine addiction. It is intentionally small and compact, so that it can be read in one sitting by people who have problems with cocaine and by their families and friends. There are a number of books available on cocaine that discuss the history of cocaine use and describe its pharmacological properties, and some of them even give treatment resources. However, very little emphasis has been placed on actual practical methods of helping people get off the drug. This book is intended to do just that. As Dr. Gold says (p. 46), "In the long run what really counts is the self-understanding that culminates in the ability to live without resort to chemical crutches of any kind." So I am directing this book to the cocaine user and to those who care about him or her, with the hope that it will also be valuable to those in counseling and other helping professions whose patients or clients are addicted to cocaine.

K. R. O'C.

Capitola, California
July 4, 1984

1

The Problem

How do you know if you have a problem with cocaine? The American Psychiatric Association's definition of cocaine abuse is:

1. Pattern of pathological use: inability to reduce or stop use; intoxication throughout the day; episodes of cocaine overdose (intoxication so severe that hallucinations and delusions occur in a clear sensorium).

2. Impairment in social or occupational functioning due to cocaine use: e.g., fights, loss of friends, absence from work, loss of job, or legal difficulties (other than due to a single arrest for possession, purchase, or sale of the substance).

3. Duration of disturbance of at least one month.

What does this mean to you? Dr. Mark Gold, a leading expert on cocaine use and treatment, uses this pragmatic working definition: "If you feel addicted, you are addicted" (*800-COCAINE,* p. 17).

If you have picked up this book, you probably are wondering whether or not you—or someone you care about—have a problem with cocaine addiction. I will not go into a lot of statistics on the cocaine problem in this country, but it is important to know that some 25 million Americans have tried cocaine at least once, and as many as 1 million have become dependent on it to the point that they cannot quit without pain, and many cannot quit at all before their addiction leads to their death. In laboratory tests, cocaine was found to be so strongly reinforcing that monkeys killed themselves to keep using it, choosing cocaine over food or sex or any other satisfaction.

Richard Ashley, in his book *Cocaine* (p. 173), says that, out of an informal survey of eighty-one users, "No one reported experiencing depression or marked craving for cocaine when their supply ran out. If they couldn't find any or couldn't afford to buy any, they simply did without." You may have found, as many others have, that this is not true for you. If you are wondering whether or not cocaine is a problem for you or someone you care about, there are some questions that you can ask yourself. They revolve around three main points, or hallmarks, of drug addiction.

The Hallmarks of Drug Addiction

The first hallmark is insatiability. Do you find that cocaine is a substance that you do not put away or save for later use? Many cocaine users have an internal sense of pressure and of insatiable need for cocaine. These are the people who can't "simply do without."

If this is the case for you, let's move along to the second hallmark, which is loss of control. This can affect your life in many ways. Perhaps you have noticed that your use of cocaine is interfering with your physical body, causing you to lose control of your memory or some other physical function or system. Perhaps you are losing control of relationships, of emotions (especially sadness and anger), or of your job and your ability to work consistently, effectively, or competently.

If you have answered yes to insatiability and yes to loss of control, let's move on to the third hallmark of cocaine addiction, which is continuing to use the drug in spite of the fact that it is causing problems. It is this third hallmark that brings most people into treatment. Often they come into the therapist's office with questions about their cocaine use as a result of pressure from a family member or friend, a spouse, or a boss. Are you jeopardizing something that is very important to you, such as a relationship or a job, and are you beginning to feel the pain involved and the risks you are taking? It is probably this pain that has brought you to consider treatment.

To illustrate, I would like to describe four people I have worked with over the past several years who experienced these hallmarks of addiction to cocaine and who have recovered.

Like many of my patients, John is self-employed, and it is this self-employment that gave him the freedom to become heavily involved with cocaine before anyone else noticed there was a problem. John is a general contractor who helps to restore people's homes. Often John would be paid in cash for his work, and instead of keeping the money to support his wife and two young children, he found himself going to his dealer's house and buying a supply of cocaine early each morning to use at work throughout the day. At first, John felt that he was more productive on cocaine, actually getting more work done. But gradually he realized that he was buying more and more cocaine, and eventually this is how he was spending all his money. Then he got involved in gambling to earn more money for his habit, which by this time was costing from $800 to $1,000 a week. This illustrates the first point of insatiability: His habit grew to where he just couldn't get enough cocaine.

The second point, loss of control, is illustrated by the fact that he kept using cocaine and working in spite of being concerned about the effect the drug was having on his heart. He could feel his heart beating very rapidly— even pounding when he tried to do heavy physical labor— and, frankly, he was scared. This is one of the ways many people have died from cocaine, by pushing their bodies beyond the limits of physical endurance. But John kept on doing cocaine. He experienced loss of control.

John was so heavily in debt that he was afraid for

himself and his family. His house had been robbed and ransacked twice—probably because he owed so much money for his cocaine and gambling. His wife was thinking of leaving him, and he loved her and didn't want to lose her. So John finally came into treatment to get help for his cocaine problem. All three hallmarks of addiction— insatiability, loss of control, and continued use in spite of adverse circumstances—were present in John's case.

A second example illustrates these same points, but with a different situation. Marium is a 28-year-old woman from an upper-middle-class East Coast family, a talented artist and businesswoman who operates a successful fashion-related business on the East Coast. Unlike many people who are addicted to cocaine, Marium does not drink alcohol at all. Her problem was a combination of cocaine and Valium, a drug she got with ease from her doctor any time she indicated problems with back pain. Marium got involved with cocaine when she was in a relationship with a man she cared about very much. They began to use cocaine together. She discovered that she had a larger and larger capacity, or tolerance, for the drug as time went on, and she also developed an uncontrollable paranoia, which was reflected in her writing. Here is one of the prose-poems she wrote during her period of active cocaine use:

> I hear the whispering, the laughing and murmuring voices. They talk about me while I listen to music. They discuss while I take a shower. Listening now, as the vague conversations revolve, I am too sorry to speak. Such an easy target.
>
> Listening, straining to confirm the sounds against my doubts. Repeatedly I hold my breath. I hope, hoping so hard, hoping until my heart pushes its pounding beats into my ears. Another chance to listen, a chance to hear. Struggling to start the chase again.

Marium spent $28,000 over approximately six months on cocaine. This strained not only her personal income but her business income as well, which caused tremendous legal complications. As I write, she has been off cocaine for several months and is doing very well. Although she is quite different from John, she showed the same symptoms of addiction: insatiability, loss of control (as demonstrated by the paranoia), and continued use in spite of adverse circumstances. She almost lost her business, and she drained a lot of her family income as well.

A third example: Josh is a 32-year-old attorney in northern California. He runs a successful law practice and he has been clean—off cocaine—for fifteen months. He was able to continue to practice law because he entered a treatment program, but many doctors, attorneys, psychologists, and other licensed professionals have not been so fortunate.

Josh was involved with cocaine to the point where he lost control of his sense of ethics and began to accept cocaine as payment for legal cases. This is not as unusual as one might think among addicted professionals. Josh developed a cocaine habit through smoking that was so severe he spent $150,000 on cocaine in eight months. He ran through a large inheritance plus the better part of the income from his law practice.

Josh began to use cocaine during court cases when he had to present his case to a jury. He felt at first that his confidence and his impact in speaking to the jury were heightened by cocaine, but eventually his performance was impaired because of his paranoia. He could never be sure whether people were really responding to him or whether he was imagining things. He began to travel with a loaded gun in his car, a habit that is not unusual for people addicted to cocaine. He considered taking his own life several times because of the depression he felt when he crashed after cocaine use. The loss of control in this case involved both anger and depression, which are equally dangerous. Through a comprehensive inpatient treatment program with very good follow-up care, Josh was able to recover and continue with his law practice. He is now helping other attorneys find help for addiction to cocaine.

Although these are three very different people from different backgrounds, they illustrate the three hallmarks of addiction very well. Their cocaine abuse is their common denominator.

I will use John and Marium and Josh as examples throughout the book. The point I would like to make here is that cocaine addiction is an illness, a disease; people who are addicted are very sick indeed. And it is a progressive illness, which means that when people are addicted to a substance, they cannot go back to recreational use.

Stages of Drug Use

Drug use progresses in five stages. The first stage is experimental use, or trying the drug out. The individual may try cigarettes or alcohol or cocaine to see what they are like and then never try them again. The use is only experimental.

The second stage is recreational or social use. This includes those who use a drug, whether it is cocaine or alcohol, on an occasional basis if it is offered to them. They do not go out and look for it. They do not experience insatiability or loss of control. They are social users.

The third stage is occasional use. This includes those who go out and look for the drug, to purchase it on their own. They may buy it to share with others, or it may only be for their own use. A woman may stay with a man who supplies her with cocaine, and their relationship may be, or become, built around their cocaine use.

The fourth stage is abuse. At this point, the user is beginning to get into trouble in one way or another related to the drug. If it is a drug like alcohol, the person may be getting picked up for traffic violations or may be acting differently from normal. Perhaps, when using the drug, the person is angrier or sadder than usual, or feels the physical effects, or has arguments with family or friends about using the drug. In some way, the drug user is beginning to feel the pain of drug use and beginning to experience loss of control. Use has become abuse.

In the fifth stage, the individual crosses over a very important line. On the other side of the line is addiction. When a person is addicted and exhibits the three hallmarks of addiction outlined earlier, that person cannot go back to experimental, social, recreational, or occasional use. He or she must abstain from all use of the drug. This is crucial. It is the philosophy that underlies this book and the philosophy that underlies successful drug and alcohol abuse treatment. No matter what study you read about in the newspapers, successful treatment of addiction means abstinence. In order to illustrate this last point, I will use a fourth example.

Steve is a 25-year-old businessman who is involved in a very successful family-owned business in northern California. He is a business success beyond his years, but he discovered that his social use of cocaine had grown into something else—something that was out of control— when he got picked up on a traffic violation and was cited for reckless driving as a result of combined cocaine and alcohol use. That was when he came in for treatment on an outpatient basis.

Three months after Steve began treatment, he decided to try one line of cocaine at a party after drinking several glasses of wine. I mention the wine because people are more likely to say yes to the offer of a line of cocaine after drinking alcohol. Steve set himself up by going to this party and accepting some alcohol, and at first he felt very good because he was able to do a couple of lines. He began to think that maybe he could use cocaine on a recreational basis again. Two days after the party, he tried some more cocaine, only this time he bought a large amount, took it home, isolated himself in his room, and did it all: several grams' worth. As a result, he became numb and paralyzed for a period, which is not an unusual occurrence with very pure cocaine, and, in fact, he almost died. This made him realize that he could not go back and do an occasional line and be okay. He had to abstain in order to recover from his addiction.

Not only did Steve need to abstain from cocaine, he also learned that he needed to abstain from drinking alcohol as well. This is not unusual for recovering cocaine addicts. When people have alcohol *even in small amounts,* they are more likely to say yes than no to a line when it is offered. Because I am interested in helping people succeed in their treatment, I recommend that they stay away from alcohol use as well. Over the years I have noted that nearly all (over 90 percent) of the people I have treated who went back to using alcohol also went back to using cocaine. This is too large a figure to ignore. We aren't just talking about statistics, we are talking about people's lives: people who get arrested; people who experience numbness and convulsions; people who suffer pain, in one way or another, as a result of their cocaine use. And, sometimes, people who die.

Cocaine and other drug abusers make a difference in our lives as well. Even if we do not have an addict in our family or among our friends, they have an effect on us that we aren't even aware of. In an article in *Newsweek,* Aug. 22, 1983, "Taking Drugs on the Job," John Brecher notes that drugs have a profound effect, both on social activity and on productivity in the workplace. As a matter of fact, it has been estimated that drug use on the job is the cause for one third less productivity among drug-abusing workers and three times as much injury and absenteeism among this population. The cost of this lack of productivity is very high as well.

And he notes (p. 52) that at least one high-tech Silicon Valley company "intentionally overproduces because it knows much of its output will be spoiled by spaced-out employees who snort their lines of coke from microscope slides." We will talk more about this in chapter 10.

The easy availability of cocaine, socially or on the job, whether you work for a mammoth corporation or are self-employed, can make getting off the drug that much more difficult. It's not easy to admit that your friends can use cocaine recreationally while for you it is a problem. As the Editors of *Rolling Stone* point out in *How to Get Off Drugs* (p. 81), "There's no right or wrong here, no good or bad. You're not a worse person for not being able to control your cocaine use. You've got a problem, that's all. But you've got to admit that." And admitting it, while still physically and mentally under the influence of cocaine, is difficult, because cocaine abuse makes objective judgments and decisions very, very hard.

2

Symptoms

Indications of cocaine abuse or addiction are as individual as the lives of those experiencing them, but with the help of my patients I have developed a list of examples of some of the problems that may be tip-offs. This list is not intended to be exhaustive or final, but it can be used as a guideline for those reading this book who may be trying to decide whether they or someone they care about have a serious problem. Of course, not all indications need to be present in any given case.

People often have a problem with cocaine, a serious problem, long before they make the connection that the difficulties they are having are a result of their drug use. Some of the connections seem subtle or difficult to grasp; others may seem obvious. Yet many people in recovery look back on their drug use and pinpoint a number of difficult times in their lives which they feel were related to their drug use, even though this was not obvious to them at the time. This is partly because of the changes in perception and judgment that occur as a result of cocaine addiction, and partly because sometimes there is a lapse or gap in time between the drug use and the occurrence of the problem. They do not necessarily occur simultaneously, so sometimes the connections are difficult to make. But they do exist, just the same.

Drug use affects clarity of thinking, and this lack of

clarity affects our daily lives in many ways. It produces a kind of crazy feeling under the surface that makes solid decision-making very difficult. Even people who appear to have a successful life generally have a problem in one or two areas. They may, for example, be successful professionally while their personal life is a shambles. They put a lot of effort into keeping up the appearance that everything is all together and running smoothly when in fact inside, deep down, they know this is not true. They are just not sure exactly why.

This is particularly common with cocaine addicts because they are often achievement-oriented and appear to be doing well in the outside world in terms of professional accomplishments while inside they know something is very wrong, and this often comes out in their personal relationships. When a cocaine addict stops using drugs, this lack of clarity in thinking and the crazy behavior that often goes with it take a while to go away. Recovering addicts need to be patient with themselves and allow time for clear thinking to come through again, giving themselves credit for the good decisions that they are increasingly making during their abstinence.

Please remember as well that the amount of the drug that is used is not the deciding factor with regard to addiction. Some people can become addicted to surprisingly small amounts of a substance. It is the problems caused by the addiction and the pain those problems cause that are the deciding factors.

Also remember that frequency of use in addiction varies widely. Some people can use as little as half a gram once a week and feel they are addicted. Other people may be binge users or periodic users and go off on a one-, two-, or three-day binge every week or two weeks, or perhaps only once every six months. What all these people have in common is that their cocaine use is causing problems in their lives.

Children often notice something amiss with a drug-abusing parent, and while they don't necessarily know that this is a result of drug use, they do pick up inconsistencies in parenting and crazy behavior. Children are particularly sensitive to these inconsistencies and to a sort of subtle neglect on the emotional level that addicted parents also recognize as a problem and generally feel badly about.

I asked several groups of patients who were coming off cocaine to give me some examples of the things they had been doing or feeling that caused them so much pain that they finally came to get help. Their lists included:

Depression, and wanting to stay in bed all the time
Isolation
Bad checks and misuse of bank card (many were unable to
    maintain a checking account at all)
Threat of jail
Suicidal feelings
Family and domestic violence
Concern for their families
Fear of violence
Fear of going crazy
Losing investments
Loss of spouse and kids
Losing a house through foreclosure
Beginning to do cocaine by themselves
Friends beginning to withhold cocaine from them
People refusing even to sell them cocaine
Loss of any kind of relationship
Doing poorly at work
Doing cocaine at work
Stealing at work or at home
Reckless or drunk driving
Cocaine blackouts
Losing a gun during a cocaine blackout
Fear of losing their health
Fear of dying as a result of the amount of cocaine used
Awareness of a rapidly pounding heart
Concern that they were going crazy
Needing to use the drug to feel normal
Needing the drug's initial rush and never being able to
    produce it again

Moving to different locations but failing to escape the drug
Thinking about cocaine all day or first thing in the morning
Misery
Loss of self-respect
Physical complications as a result of cocaine use, including
    septile defects, chronic sinus conditions, and aches and
    pains in the joints
Increased tolerance, so that more and more of the drug
    is used
Decreased tolerance, so that even a small amount causes
    numbness or convulsions
Unclear thinking
Violently protecting the drug supply
Binge use
Arguments over using or not using the drug
Accidents while using cocaine or as a result of using cocaine
    (I have seen several people who work with tools cutting
    off portions of their fingers as a result of being hung over
    from cocaine and alcohol)
Rationalization and blaming their own faults on other people
Guilt
Sneaking or lying for cocaine
Beginning to become very concerned over having enough
Desiring to get high with cocaine more and more frequently

This is a long list, but perhaps it will help you organize
your thoughts about your own drug use. It may bring
difficulties to your attention that you hadn't connected
with cocaine. If you are concerned—and you must be, to
have picked up this book—sit down and make your own
list. You may be surprised at just how much of a difference cocaine has made in your life.

3

Treatment Philosophy

If my description has convinced you that you or someone you love does have a problem with cocaine, what do you do now?

All four people described in the last chapter were children of alcoholics. That is to say, at least one parent in each case drank alcohol to excess at some point. In fact, more than 90 percent of the patients I have treated for cocaine abuse have at least one parent who has had a problem with a substance, usually alcohol, at some time. This means that people with at least one parent with a substance abuse problem are more likely to develop a similar problem. It's easy to say, "I'll never be like them," in looking at an alcoholic parent, but not as easy to follow through. It is useful to know that many of the patterns learned in childhood in growing up in an alcoholic's family are repeated until treatment changes the picture. So the first step is to acknowledge that this pattern exists.

A second pattern most often present in those who develop a problem with cocaine is a grief pattern. In taking the histories of these people, I found that heavy cocaine use is often preceded by a loss of some kind—a relationship, a job—that precipitated feelings of sadness or depression. Cocaine is often used by people as the easiest available medication to treat depression and sadness. It is ineffective, though, because its effect in the body lasts such a short time. People who are depressed and use cocaine experience greater depression with prolonged use and a greater amount of down time and larger emotional crashes after such use. So please go back over your life and examine it for losses and see how those losses may have tied in with increased cocaine use.

The next pattern is that many cocaine addicts have a long-term pattern of drug use and abuse. Many of us who are now in our thirties grew up with a very heavily drug-oriented culture in the 1960s. It is not unusual for people to say that they began to use drugs at 11, 12, or 13 years of age, starting with tobacco and going on to alcohol and marijuana, and then to pills and speed and sometimes hallucinogens, and later to cocaine. They graduated from the cheap stuff and went into the more expensive drugs as they became financially more successful in their lives and wanted to reward themselves. Many people have been high on one drug or another almost continuously since about age 13. It is important to know that this affects judgment, perception, and normal emotional development.

Drug use, especially cocaine use, affects judgment and perception in a profound way. Crazy behaviors, like paranoid fears, seem normal with cocaine in your system. This is true even if you have not used cocaine recently but have used it within, say, thirty days. This is why I ask my patients to avoid making important decisions in their lives until they have been completely clean and sober for at least sixty days. If you have been high on one thing or another since age 13 or 14, you have never had clear judgment, and your life probably reflects this. Please take this opportunity to go over your history of drug use and take a look at the pattern of judgments and decision-making during that time.

Normal emotional growth and development are often arrested or retarded as a result of drug use. If you have been using drugs since age 13 or 14, then emotionally you may feel that you are a teenager, and you may act like one. Recovery from cocaine addiction will involve a lot of normal growth and development that you have not yet had a chance to experience. In this respect, as in many others, recovery from cocaine addiction can be a gift, a gift of living fully and experiencing yourself fully as a complete human being.

Arrested growth and development often involve a pattern of sexual behavior problems. Marium, who was mentioned earlier in this book, was active sexually from the age of 13. But when she looked back at many of her sexual experiences, she would rather have passed them up. This is not unusual in recovery, especially for women, many of whom have sold or traded sex for drugs. For very young women or women who do not work outside the home, sex may seem to them to be the obvious way to get the cocaine they want and come to feel they need. The three-way relationship of woman, man, and cocaine does nothing for either person's self-confidence, however, and the woman who begins using coke as part of a relationship often finds that she still has the problem after her lover or husband has gone. In fact, she has more problems than she did before, and cocaine, even if she can get it, is by this time less and less help. Men are also doubly dependent, on the drug and on the dealer from whom they get the drug, and of course it is twice as expensive to supply two habits.

It is also not unusual for the cocaine addict not to remember things that have happened. Events that involve sexuality or strong emotions like sadness or anger may be blacked out. Marium has many blanks in her memory of her past life and feels as if she lived another life "back there." Because cocaine in and of itself causes a certain amount of memory loss, many people have difficulty memorizing things during their heavy cocaine use, which of course further involves their job or school performance.

The last pattern I am going to mention is the increasing alcohol use common with people who develop a cocaine problem. Often people go from being social drinkers to developing a real problem with alcohol in conjunction with the use of cocaine. It is not unusual for men especially to tell me how they have polished off a whole case of beer in the course of a day on a cocaine binge. So in checking over your patterns, notice any changes you have made in your alcohol use in conjunction with cocaine. Or, like Marium, you may have used other drugs as a way of bringing you down so you could crash or get some rest after a cocaine binge, drugs like Quaaludes and Valium and other downers.

As you can see, cocaine addiction has physical, intellectual, and emotional effects on your life. It also has spiritual effects, as I will discuss in the next chapter.

4

Cocaine and Its Effects

Although researchers do not agree on how it happens, those of us who work with addicts know that cocaine affects users on all four levels: body, mind, emotions, and spirit.

Effects at the Physical Level

The physical effects lay the foundation for the mental, emotional, and spiritual ones, and the most serious physical effect, being seen more and more frequently in emergency rooms, is death. Although 1984 statistics are not yet available, emergency-room clinicians are seeing an increase of some 300 percent in cocaine-related deaths since 1979. Of course this is an approximate figure, as tests for cocaine in the system are not routine in most hospitals.

Cocaine and Death

Many deaths from cocaine involve people who die in car crashes as a result of driving under the influence of cocaine, often combined with alcohol. Please note that I do not call these "accidents" but deliberately refer to them as "crashes," to emphasize that these deaths have a cause; they are *not* accidental. Cocaine induces a sense of confidence, and people who use it and drink feel that they can handle a car in spite of the cocaine and alcohol in their bodies. But the effects of the alcohol long outlast the effects of the cocaine. When the cocaine wears off, the individual is left drunk behind the wheel.

The second cause of death from cocaine is overdosing. This is becoming more frequent because the supply of cocaine available on the street is increasing, and the price is going down. Coca leaves take several years to harvest. A large crop was planted several years ago and is now available. There are more cocaine-related deaths because there is more cocaine, and it is purer. Pure cocaine is more likely to cause paralysis, numbness, and convulsions. It is a very strong drug. There have been deaths as a result of intranasal use, intravenous use, and freebase use. Contrary to street myths, all three modes of entry can produce death.

I should mention several basic facts about cocaine and how it is used, although I am assuming that most people who read this book know these things already. I am not going into detail on this topic, because you can get this information from other books, especially Dr. Mark Gold's *800-COCAINE.*

People do die from intranasal cocaine, or snorting. Intranasal use is drawing cocaine into the nostrils, and the cocaine which is used in this way is a white, powdery substance called cocaine hydrochloride.

Freebasing also involves cocaine hydrochloride, only it is mixed with ether in a petri dish to create a pasty substance that is heated to evaporate the ether, leaving unadulterated cocaine. Small amounts can then be placed in the neck of a special pipe and smoked at a high temperature over a torch. Using cocaine in this way creates a very intense rush. Of course, one of the dangers involved in smoking cocaine is death as a result of an explosion or fire—as Richard Pryor was injured—although the cocaine smoke is very damaging to the lungs also.

The third way to take cocaine is, of course, intrave-nously, with a needle. Cocaine hydrochloride—street co-caine—can be dissolved in water and drawn up into a syringe. A vein is tied off and the cocaine injected directly into it. Taking cocaine in this way will create an immediate high, or rush, which lasts up to ten minutes. The rush is so intense and so quick that users will often inject them-selves over the course of a night many, many times to keep creating that rush effect.

Intravenous use of cocaine can lead to various types of bacterial and viral infections because of using a dirty needle. And because intravenous use creates such an immediate effect and such a large rush, death can occur very quickly from ventricular fibrillation or cardiac arrest. Also, a user with a weak blood vessel in the brain can die from a breakage of that vessel—or survive that trauma but live with the impairments of a stroke. I am talking about young people here, who have no other indication of health problems, but in whom cocaine abuse leads inevitably to damage or death.

Cocaine also affects the heat-regulating mechanism, so that the body increases its temperature. This is caused by constriction of the blood vessels and decreased heat radiation. Grand mal convulsions can be triggered by cocaine use, particularly very pure cocaine, and death can occur from suffering one seizure after another and not getting medical help soon enough.

Of course, people who have heart problems such as angina are at a very high risk when they use cocaine, because their coronary blood flow is already damaged. Diabetics are also at an increased risk of death, because the use of cocaine unbalances their blood sugar level so much that they may go into a coma and die.

As I noted earlier, people also die from violence sec-ondary to cocaine use, as a result of paranoia and imag-ined persecution. Traveling with guns or weapons is not unusual, and violence can be triggered by very small events. Also, there have been many industrial accidents, such as severed fingers or worse, involving people who work with machinery because they were either on cocaine or coming off of it and were experiencing impaired judgment and perception. These workers can also endanger those around them. John Brecher (p. 55) quotes a construction union leader in California, who says, "I just leave the job when the guys are dopers. Would you want to work on a 14-story building knowing the guy with the blowtorch next to you is doing drugs?"

The paranoia associated with the more acute stages of abuse often results in thoughts—and sometimes actions—of suicide, and an undetermined number of apparent suicides or accidental deaths are undoubtedly a result of cocaine depression. A less obvious form of suicide occurs when health and existing medical conditions are neglected until the illness is irreversible. Malnutrition and lack of sleep can cause emotional imbalance even without cocaine, and they are certainly factors in the perceptual difficulties of cocaine addicts. Cocaine paranoia can also result in violence to others who appear threatening to the addict, from partners to suppliers to police officers. Josh was not unusual in carrying a gun during his cocaine abuse. Again, because medical personnel are often not knowledgeable about the effects of cocaine addiction, our statistics on the real damage done by this drug are undoubtedly highly inaccurate.

For those who smuggle cocaine, a cause of death is body packing, which is swallowing or otherwise placing in one or more body cavities large quantities of cocaine, usually in a plastic bag. If the package breaks and the cocaine is absorbed by the body, the smuggler can die very quickly.

Another cause of death is anorexia. Some women use cocaine before a party so they won't eat and so that they will feel confident about their appearance. I have seen many cases of extreme weight loss and appetite loss resulting from cocaine use. This can be very dangerous. It is usually women who use cocaine as a diet aid, because women are expected to be slim and attractive. I will discuss women's place in the world of cocaine use in chapter 10, but I would like to point out here that it is ironic for both women and men that cocaine use has often destroyed the very careers and relationships it was originally used to assist.

Cocaine and Nutrition

We are learning more about cocaine and its effects on nutrition, so I am including a number of suggested nutritional supplements. *Please bear in mind that whenever the physical effects of cocaine are of concern, you should always consult a physician,* one whom you trust enough to be honest about your condition. Try to make sure that this person has been trained to treat substance abuse and knows the physical complications of cocaine use and addiction. Again, remember that not all health care providers get substance treatment information as part of their training. A doctor or nurse familiar with susbtance addiction can give you better care.

There are several useful tips included in Michael Weiner's *Getting Off Cocaine,* and you may find it worthwhile to read this book, especially the sections on improving your nutritional status and correcting deficiencies resulting from cocaine abuse. I will not go into detail about supplements but will list a few points here.

L-tryptophan, an amino acid, has been helpful to many people coming off cocaine because it has the physical effect of relaxing them and helping them to get some sleep, which is often a problem in early recovery, and because it has a neurochemical effect in reducing drug hunger. In addition, I recommend a multivitamin and mineral supplement, one that includes zinc, manganese, chromium, and magnesium, a B-complex, and extra C as well. I will discuss supplements further on in this section under "Recommendations," but I want to note here that recovering addicts are often deficient in vitamins and minerals because of poor eating and sleeping habits; they were more interested in doing cocaine than anything else.

One of the stress factors that sets people up for using cocaine again and again has to do with overburdening the body. It is very important to have a good diet, get enough sleep, and greatly reduce your intake of caffeine and, if possible, tobacco while recovering from cocaine addiction. Give yourself not only enough food but the right kinds. Stay away from junk food. Take care of your body, because otherwise the cycle of stress that includes depleting the body of rest and adequate nutrition will feed right back into the cocaine cycle. If the body is not treated well, it crashes, much like the crash of low energy and depression after cocaine use. The feelings of depression and low energy that come when people don't eat enough or get enough sleep often remind them of the times that preceded cocaine binges and may act as a fuse or trigger.

The role of exercise is important also. Again, wait at least five days after doing the drug before you get involved in any kind of physical activity. Aerobic exercise is particularly beneficial, partly because it helps counteract the depression that is often present at this time. (There is a lot of literature to support this.) Exercise also helps to regulate the body in order to get it back on a sound, stable cycle and avoid the large swings in energy that characterize the cocaine use cycle. These swings in energy and mood must be avoided.

Cocaine and Sex

The role of cocaine in sex is one that is certainly joked about and to some degree glamorized, but it is very poorly understood from a physiological standpoint. One of the things that we do know about cocaine is that only one use for cocaine is medically approved in the United States: as a topical anesthetic—that is to say, to make one numb. It is not surprising, then, that women, especially, notice that they stop having physical sensations in their pelvic region when they are using cocaine, and so many women do not like to have sex during drug use. It is also why many women develop secondary sexual difficulties in responding to a partner in early recovery. Dr. Gold (p. 19) notes that many women have found that men "become so self-absorbed when they have sex while on cocaine that they forget about their partner and her needs." He says that cocaine "may be conceptualized as a partner in masturbation." Fortunately, with education about the effects of cocaine, most women can reverse their difficulties over time.

Men too discover problems after prolonged and heavy cocaine use. At first, the cocaine seems like a lot of fun and enhances sexuality, and many men have introduced their wives or lovers to cocaine in order to improve their sex lives. But when the cocaine use gets to the point where tolerance increases and addiction sets in, either sex becomes of secondary interest to the use of the drug itself, or the man becomes impotent. This is also reversible simply by staying away from the drug.

Cocaine's reputation as an aphrodisiac or enhancer of sexual performance has undoubtedly led many to experiment with it who would not have done so otherwise. It is important for casual users and people who have not yet tried cocaine to understand that the sexual effects of cocaine are as temporary as the confident highs. When these are gone, the habit is still there, and the user now has more problems with relationships, whether personal or business, than before.

Cocaine and Pregnancy

There are very few data on the effects of cocaine during pregnancy, and we need good research in this area very badly. To some extent we can draw from our research on the fetal alcohol syndrome and on alcohol and its effects on the fetus in general. Also, we can draw on clinical knowledge from doctors who have been seeing cocaine-addicted women over the past several years. I have seen too many cases of first-trimester miscarriage to ignore the fact that this might be a frequent complication of cocaine use during early pregnancy. For this reason, I recommend that women patients stay off cocaine for a year before attempting to get pregnant, with at least six months' abstinence for men. More and more, research in the area of alcohol abuse shows that the health of both father and mother affects the health of the fetus. Cocaine is a drug that has profound effects on the nervous, cardiac, and respiratory systems. How could this not affect a developing fetus?

It would also seem obvious that the poor nutrition and sleeping habits of the cocaine abuser would be damaging to the fetus as well as to the body of the mother. An infant needs a healthy mother, both before and after birth, and a woman who is using cocaine so frequently that her life is built around it is not likely to have the energy or the patience to care for an infant or a young child. If cocaine is so important to you that you feel you must use it during pregnancy, I recommend that you seek treatment, because this is a good indication that your cocaine use has become a problem.

Cocaine and Brain Damage

Most cases of brain damage that I see on an outpatient basis connected to cocaine use are transient or temporary. However, some long-term effects can include migraine headaches and increased risk of stroke, especially for those people on birth control pills. If you are experiencing frequent headaches, a neurologist should be consulted. Transient damage includes memory loss, especially recent memories of events and information. The other damage I often see is concentration impairment, where people have trouble sitting down and absorbing information. In fact, several months of treatment often pass before most people can start reading a whole book again. This is one of the reasons why I have kept this book so short.

Recommendations

I would like to make three general recommendations to help build up your physical health as part of your early recovery program from cocaine addiction—particularly during the first thirty days. Again, always check with your physician before you start any new health program, including this one.

1. Treat your body well. This includes rest at night, because sufficient sleep is very important at this time. You will also find that you are more tired than usual; this is normal in the early recovery process from cocaine addiction. Accept this need for extra sleep and allow for it. Look at this time as one of catching up on your rest just as you would if you were recovering from a bad case of the flu.

2. Maintain a constant physical energy level. I am referring to your level of energy output throughout the day, because one of the things that happens to people who develop cocaine problems is that they get used to experiencing uneven energy levels and to duplicating the cocaine high-and-crash cycle constantly during the day. As I said earlier, it is important to stabilize the output of energy; otherwise the body gets the message in the slower or depressed part of the cycle that it needs more cocaine in order to pick itself up, and then it is all too easy to resume your destructive drug habits. This cycle must be stopped by taking care of your body.

In order to maintain a proper energy level, it is important to see that certain vitamins, amino acids, and minerals that are depleted as a result of cocaine use are now replaced. Start with a good multivitamin that has a mineral supplement included. Whatever you take, please make sure that it contains a large dose of the B-complex and C vitamins and the minerals zinc, magnesium, manganese, and chromium. These are very important to stabilize the blood sugar level—and therefore the energy level—throughout the day. In addition, cocaine users are usually deficient in minerals like zinc and manganese, and these must be replaced. In taking a multivitamin, do not take extra vitamin A because cocaine contains it, and it is one of the vitamins that can be overdone, resulting in toxic side effects, so only take the amount that is present in the multiple vitamin. You may want to take vitamins twice a day, with meals, the first thirty days of recovery, in order to make up for some of your deficiencies.

The role of amino acids is also important in cocaine recovery. Some of the research indicates that the amino acids L-tryptophan and tyrosine are deficient in cocaine users, and replacing these substances can actually reduce your desire for cocaine. I recommend that you take the L-tryptophan before bedtime, one 500mg tablet for every 75 pounds of body weight. You should take it only at bedtime because some people get very drowsy when using it, and that isn't helpful during the day. Tyrosine is also helpful; it occurs in a mixed amino acid supplement. These can be found at health food stores and usually contain 15 to 17 amino acids in one formula. Consider taking one of these in the morning with your multivitamin supplement.

3. Develop an exercise program. Exercise is also very important in early recovery from cocaine addiction, particularly aerobic exercise. But please do not exercise until you have been off cocaine at least five days, because of the stress on your heart. As I pointed out earlier, exercising while on cocaine can be very dangerous, and this includes strenuous activity on the job. Also remember that soaking in a Jacuzzi or hot tub is not recommended because it increases blood pressure and cardiac output. Wait at least five days. When you do begin to exercise, swimming, bicycling, and jogging, or brisk walks or hikes, are all excellent activities. Wait at least seven days before beginning extremely strenuous activities such as racquetball. Take it easy on yourself at this time, and work into an exercise program gradually.

Effects at the Mental Level

Some of the information under mental level recovery has already been covered under the section "Cocaine and Brain Damage." Most of the brain damage I see, as I have noted, is of a transient or temporary nature. People often find that they have difficulty with their recent memory function, such as remembering telephone numbers or the right exit off the freeway to get to the doctor's office. These memory losses rarely last more than thirty days, so don't worry too much about them. Concentration problems are also very common and go hand in hand with the feeling of restlessness.

Mental attitude is very important in recovery from cocaine addiction. Be sure to read chapter 6 on behavioral interventions, which is the core of this treatment program, because it addresses the mental attitude and covers areas of cognitive restructuring and the changing of thought patterns and ways of thinking that are so important to recovery. It is important to include in your life anything that promotes a stable, optimistic mental set. Thoughts like "Nobody cares about anybody else in this world, so it's not worth trying to be nice to people because people are basically out to get each other" are typical of the mental set often found as a result of cocaine use. It is important to change these thoughts, because the thoughts affect the emotions. The cycle goes like this: Thoughts lead to feelings; feelings lead to physical states; physical states lead to drug drives; drug drives lead to drug urges; and drug urges lead to drug-related behavior (i.e., getting the drug and using it). You can see from this that thoughts are very powerful and lead to behavior and decision-making that can affect your health and the quality of your life. Thoughts and emotions are very closely tied. This is the basis for the behavioral aspect of this program.

Effects at the Emotional Level

The effect of cocaine use on the emotions is a profound one. Approximately 65 percent of the patients I have treated for cocaine addiction have seriously considered suicide at least once during their cocaine use cycle. Over half of these people have actually created a plan to kill themselves—such as taking a gun with them in the car, keeping loaded weapons around constantly, or thinking of jumping off a bridge—in general, feeling very hopeless about themselves and the world. They want to "shut it all off," as one of my patients put it. Thus, the negative mind-set we discussed earlier affects the emotions and the feelings. Depression is very common; this is one reason why medical treatment is so important in early recovery. It may be helpful to use antidepressant medication for a short time to elevate the emotional mood and the energy level, both of which contribute to the depression. Depression is a very serious problem, and the risk of suicide can also be real at this time. If someone with a cocaine problem is talking about suicide, *please take the person seriously!*

The second most prevalent emotion found in people who do cocaine is anger or rage, escalating into an uncontrollable situation where physical violence is possible. I'm talking about people who are not normally violent, but who become violent as a result of their cocaine use. At some level cocaine gives many people permission to take the lid off their rage and to express it in destructive ways. I have seen too many cases of domestic violence involving wife or child beating or destruction of property to take this lightly. It is a serious possibility. Again, like depression, the rage is treated by getting off cocaine. And when feelings have escalated to the point of suicide or uncontrollable rage, addicts need to be hospitalized for at least thirty days. Such people cannot usually be treated in an outpatient setting, even one where they spend ten to twelve hours a week in the program.

I have said that many people get involved in taking cocaine heavily after some kind of loss. It is not unusual for clients to say that their heavy cocaine use followed the death of someone they cared about, a divorce, breaking up with a lover, or some other traumatic event that involved the need to work through the grief process. Often people get involved in taking cocaine as a way of numbing feelings and decreasing the feelings of sadness and grief that are inevitable in such a situation. Cocaine simply delays the grief process, and people who take cocaine for this reason find that when they quit they still need to work through the loss and the grief, and this is an important part of their treatment program. The original emotions of sadness or grief become magnified by being suppressed, and often these feelings become very strong immediately after these people stop using cocaine.

For example, Marium began to take cocaine heavily after breaking up with the lover she had been living with for some years. This delayed the depression and sadness, but the feelings did not go away. And so every time a sad feeling came up, she would take cocaine to suppress it. When she finally withdrew from cocaine use she found that there was no shortcut. She still needed to deal with the grief process so she could move on to other things in her life. This involved making a commitment to living, a commitment that is basic to successful treatment. Many people, and not only cocaine abusers, have not made this commitment to staying alive, and they can easily get involved through drug use in a cycle downward toward death. Again, I would like to emphasize that all levels of cocaine impairment—physical, mental, emotional, and spiritual—interact, and in this case the emotional and spiritual levels are especially involved, although the physical effects of cocaine addiction and the mental effects of choosing to use cocaine to deaden emotional pain are of course also involved. It is particularly important to have a support network during early recovery where irrational and past impulses will be understood for what they are, a result of cocaine addiction. It is also important at this time to take care of yourself emotionally and to accept that you are what you are and have done what you have done, and then go on to create a more satisfactory life for yourself.

Again, I would like to encourage you to treat your body well also, as physical conditions can have a strong effect on mental and emotional states. Maintaining a balance will help you avoid the urge to return to cocaine use, and this balance is affected, as I have said before, by blood sugar level, fatigue, depression, or bitterness. Finding this balance is often aided by finding your spiritual foundation as well.

Effects at the Spiritual Level

The spiritual level is often ignored in the treatment of cocaine addicts, but the effects of cocaine on spiritual life need to be recognized. The word "spiritual" means different things to different people. When I use the word I do not necessarily mean the religious, churchgoing sense, I mean a personal-spiritual sense that is individual to you and different for each of us. For some people, finding their spiritual base means getting back into contact with nature and spending more time in peaceful, natural settings where they are able to get in touch with themselves and find a sense of peace within. It is that feeling of peace and serenity that is important; how you find it is up to you. Some people use relaxation techniques and meditation, which can be very effective. In the next chapter I will talk about the role of trance in cocaine addiction, and how it can be used in treatment. The main thing is to find a way to relax and find that peaceful place within yourself. This can be as simple as sitting in a quiet environment in a comfortable chair and breathing in and out very deeply and slowly, noticing the rhythm of your breathing and how it relaxes your body.

Most people who get involved with using cocaine heavily treat life as if it were a short fast sprint. In a short race, you need to gear up very quickly because the race will be over very fast, and the burnout is quick and severe. Life is really much more like a cross-country run and is best treated as such. People who learn to pace themselves through life are less likely to burn out at an early age. Many of the patients I see who develop cocaine addiction have a belief that they are going to die at about age 30, and they act out this belief in their lives by treating their minds and bodies as if they were not going to last. In fact, with heavy cocaine use the mind and body will not last long, so be aware of the quality of your life and the way you are treating yourself. If life for you is a long-distance run, you need to pace yourself and take time to gear up and stretch out and find a pace that is stable and steady and consistent throughout life.

Often in the period of early recovery, people discover that their cocaine addiction may actually be viewed as a gift. This sounds strange at first, but actually an addiction can be a wonderful gift that we should open and examine to find the amazing and exciting things we can discover about ourselves as our recovery progresses. This will make our lives much richer and higher in quality and, in short, worth living well.

Often people in recovery from cocaine addiction get involved in helping other people, and this is part of the gift of recovery. They are not only helping those others but helping themselves to maintain their recovery. This is also a time when people reexamine things about themselves that go way back. For example, they often do a values inventory. They go back to an early age to determine what values they learned from their parents, family, and close friends, and then they decide which of those values they will keep, which ones they want to change in their recovery, and, perhaps, which new values they want to add. This value clarification inventory process is a very useful tool in recovery because it helps people to perceive their cocaine addiction and their new understanding of themselves as a gift, a way of lending more richness to life.

This is also a time when many of my patients make radical changes in their way of living. I often tell them that quitting cocaine is 40 percent of the recovery process and the other 60 percent is changing their life-style in order to stay clean. The Editors of *Rolling Stone* comment in *How to Get Off Drugs* (p. 22):

> The influence of drugs on social activity is complex, for the setting (where and with whom drugs are used) is an important aspect of drug-taking. Users often choose friends because of the drugs they use, or choose to use drugs because it is the practice of their friends.

In the next two chapters I will discuss how drug use is incorporated into the individual's life-style and how changes in life-style can help lessen the chances of returning to drugs.

5

The Role of Trance
in the Recovery Process

Consider the example of Josh, the attorney who made an excellent recovery from his cocaine addiction over a fifteen-month period. Josh was a heavy user. He was a freebaser of cocaine, spending a total of several hundred thousand dollars on his addiction. He came into my office for an evaluation, and I recommended that he go into a thirty-day inpatient hospital program, which he did. He followed up with intensive therapy after being discharged, and he also attends a Cocaine Anonymous group. These are the keys to his recovery. It is interesting to note, however, that Josh, like many people addicted to cocaine, spent a good part of his life in a trance, and this trance was part of his cycle of cocaine use. It will be helpful to examine how he experienced this trance, and how we used the trance state as a way to help him in his recovery.

Josh was going through a number of transitions in his life, including a relatively new marriage, a baby on the way, and a high-volume successful law practice that he had inherited when his father died about two years before. In short, he felt a lot of pressure on him, and he was a relatively recent law school graduate. This is when Josh's cocaine use changed from recreational to heavy.

Josh also illustrates a point that we discussed in chapter 4 in the section "Effects at the Emotional Level," because he was doing the cocaine partly because of his depression over his father's death and the resulting pressures on him. If Josh had a tough day at the office, he would go out for lunch with Roger, a friend of his who was also a lawyer and also did cocaine, and they would have one or two beers with their meal. (I'm mentioning the alcohol because, as I indicated earlier, even small amounts of alcohol can set people up to want some cocaine.) Josh and Roger would decide about three times a week, after having those beers, to go over to their dealer's house and buy some cocaine and freebase it. Josh had a lot of difficulty remembering exactly what happened on these occasions. We put together the events in subsequent therapy sessions, but Josh's lack of memory has to do with the fact that he was in a trance from the time he got to the lunch table at the restaurant.

In this state of trance the mind is focused or narrowed on only one thing. He already had the idea in his mind that he was going to do cocaine, before he even sat down for lunch, so his mind focused, just as he could have concentrated on any other idea or topic. This is a trance state. As a result of his trance, Josh would get up, go to the telephone, and dial his dealer's number so automatically that he did not even have to think about it. It was as if he were a robot on automatic. The automatic nature of his actions is a good tip-off of the trance state. After dialing the number, he would go with Roger to the dealer's house.

Josh also does not remember any of these trips, because he was on automatic. We all have such experiences, which are often called road hypnosis, such as getting into the car in the morning and making all the right moves to get to work. Often we remember getting into the car, and getting to the destination, but nothing in between. We were in a trance.

As part of his recovery process, Josh learned to redirect his trance state and to identify when he was in it. He learned that because of a combination of events, including the trance state and his conditioning, he had to avoid some situations, such as the restaurants where he and his friend used to meet. He was conditioned to think about cocaine when he thought about those restaurants, so going there was a poor idea for him, no matter why he went or who he was with. (His conditioning might also have been to Roger's name, or the name of a bar, or any other cue that would set off the urge for cocaine.) This conditioning, or establishing a pattern, combines with the trance state to create a very powerful mind-set. This is why it is important for people in recovery from cocaine addiction to identify their regular patterns of cocaine use—in other words, the events, places, people, and moods that preceded getting the cocaine—and to avoid them, because these are setups for dangerous situations. Such very strong reinforcers for cocaine use *must be avoided at all costs.*

I taught Josh how to identify a trance state in himself and how to redirect it. I taught him first that he could change his desire for cocaine by changing his mental and physiological state with a technique that I have developed that I call PRE, or Psychophysiological Re-Education.

If your mind gets an idea or a thought like "Gee, wouldn't some cocaine be nice," the next step is the feeling that goes along with it: "Oh, yes, I remember what it was like when I first did cocaine. It was a rush feeling and I liked it. I'd like some more." The next step is drug desire, or the thought, "Gee, I'd like to try some again." The next step is a physical change in the body called drug hunger, where the body actually begins to behave as if it already had the drug when in fact the drug hasn't been taken yet. At this point, most people are on the phone to their dealer. In the case of cocaine, the signs of this condition include an increased pulse rate, a dry mouth, changes in the pupils, a feeling of energy or in some cases euphoria, and sometimes a sense of sexual excitement. The final step after drug hunger is actually getting the drug, a change in behavior. So we follow the cycle from a thought, to a feeling, to drug desire, to drug hunger, and to behavior. It is helpful to know that this is a predictable chain of events, because you can stop at any link in the chain.

It is *most effective* to stop this chain of events at the thought stage. In other words, when the thought comes into your mind, "Gee, wouldn't some cocaine be nice," or when someone mentions the word "cocaine," it is important to stop the process. This can be done by learning how to put yourself into a very relaxed state of being. This takes practice but can be achieved by anyone. You might sit down in a comfortable chair and do some deep, slow breathing and think about something that is relaxing to you—perhaps a vacation, or just lying in the sun—some mental scene that is either visual or auditory or both that makes you feel relaxed. Notice that your pulse rate will go down when you begin to feel relaxed, decreasing by as much as ten to fifty beats per minute. This is an important point because if your mind, just by thinking of a relaxing situation, can reduce your pulse rate, that means your mind has a profound effect on your body and the way it responds physically. When your pulse rate is lower and you are feeling relaxed, it is impossible to have an urge for cocaine. This is worth repeating: You cannot have an urge to do cocaine when you are relaxed and have a low pulse rate.

Practice this relaxation exercise frequently during the day so that you train yourself to become relaxed quickly, deeply, and effectively. Relaxing is a skill, and it can be learned with practice like any other skill. Whenever someone mentions cocaine, or you think about cocaine, relax immediately. Make your breathing deeper and slower, think about a relaxing situation or place, and reduce your pulse rate. You will find that this works every time to cut off any urge to do cocaine. Many people have successfully used this technique for years.

You can use PRE anywhere along the thought-feeling-desire-urge-behavior chain, but it is easiest to do at the beginning, at the thought stage. So practice the technique. You can do yourself a big favor and save yourself a lot of torment and anguish.

Josh found that any time he thought about cocaine, or when it was mentioned, he could stop having urges by using the PRE technique, and the number of urges decreased every day, until he had absolutely *no* urges to do cocaine. And he found that the number of thoughts about cocaine per day decreased, until he rarely thought about it at all.

This technique is especially useful and powerful because you can practice it on yourself. It puts you in control. You will notice that your urges go away eventually, and that even your thoughts about cocaine decrease and eventually go away. You can measure your progress over days and weeks yourself. All you need to do is commit yourself to practicing the technique on a regular basis. Any work that you may have done in the past in the area of meditation or self-hypnosis or relaxation techniques will be helpful in applying relaxation and allow you to be more confident more quickly. Some people even purchase audio tapes about relaxation or self-hypnosis that they listen to during the day to help them practice relaxing skills. Learn this technique well, because when you get good at it, you can even use it in surprise situations, such as when you go to someone's house and he or she pulls out some cocaine, or you see a movie or a news report that gets your thoughts going about cocaine. Just practice your relaxation technique and check those thoughts out. You are in control.

6

Behavioral Techniques in the Treatment of Cocaine Addiction

Psychologists have learned other techniques in the past forty years in the area of behavioral treatment that are very helpful in recovering from cocaine addiction. Relaxation techniques and knowledge about conditioning and reinforcement were discussed in the last chapter, and these are very helpful in avoiding high-risk situations or handling surprise situations involving cocaine. You can avoid many situations that would otherwise have been a threat to your new-found resistance to cocaine by being aware of the objects, situations, people, or moods that trigger off a drug urge.

Cue Reduction

In chapter 5, we talked about the role of thoughts in the chain of events leading to cocaine use and detailed the chain itself, which starts with a thought, leading to a feeling, which then leads to a drug desire, then a drug urge, and then to the behavior of taking the drug. I stressed that it is best to stop this chain of events at the thought stage and insisted that you avoid those cues—situations, thoughts, or people—that reminded you of doing cocaine. You remember that, for Josh, going to lunch at certain restaurants was a cue, so he needed to stay away from those restaurants. He couldn't even afford to think about their names, because that might remind him about cocaine and set up the chain that would lead him to do the drug again.

Josh also needed to avoid his friend Roger, with whom he shared those lunches and the cocaine—for dessert, if you will. Certain friends can be cues. This can be a hard piece of information to accept, but by accepting it you will avoid a lot of pain and difficult situations.

If most of your friends are cues, it is extremely important for you to consider inpatient or residential treatment rather than an outpatient program. It is important for you to have a support system of people who are clean and able to support you in staying away from doing cocaine, rather than what I call a sabotage system, people who will try to get you involved with doing cocaine again. So, please, carefully evaluate the people around you and determine which of them are cues. Even the mention of certain people's names can set up a feeling of wanting to do cocaine, so it is important to avoid thinking about their names or faces.

Many things can be cues, and some of the ones that have appeared frequently in my practice are:

Names for cocaine. It is important to stay away from words that people might mention, such as toot, blow, lady, and snow.

Places. You know best which places you should avoid: those homes where cocaine is available, your dealer's, certain restaurants and bars where you know cocaine is easily accessible, perhaps even your place of employment. Carefully examine your work situation. You may need to change jobs in order to recover.

Moods. We talked about feelings of sadness or depression in the section "Effects at the Emotional Level." Many people use cocaine as a pick-me-up when they are in a down mood. Even happy moods may be cues for those who have been using cocaine as a reward for achievement.

Sex. Some people connect cocaine very closely with sex. Most often I find this in shooters, because often sexual activities are connected with their cocaine use. Sex for sale or sex in hotel room situations can often be a cue also.

Travel. Being on the road for business or pleasure can be a cue for cocaine use.

Paraphernalia. This is a big cue for just about everybody. It is very important to get rid of your bullets, bindles, mirrors, straws, and other implements, including scales, because these are all strong cues.

Your home. It is important to rearrange certain areas of your house if you have used those areas repeatedly for cocaine use. Many people find themselves redecorating a room where they frequently used cocaine in order to see it as a different place, not connected with cocaine anymore. Or you may even need to move.

Alcohol. Alcohol use is a very frequent cocaine cue because alcohol is a permission-giver. As I have said before, people are more likely to say yes than no to a line after drinking even small amounts of alcohol.

Recreational activities. Certain activities, such as skiing, have been connected with cocaine use.

Work situations. For some people, certain types of high-pressure situations are connected with cocaine use. A salesman, for example, may often start doing cocaine before a sales talk, or an attorney before a jury presentation. Practice, combined with your new relaxation skills, will help you handle these situations confidently without resorting to cocaine.

This list is not intended to be exhaustive, it is just some ideas to get you started on developing a cue list of your own. Start with the things that are mild cues for cocaine use and move on to the moderate and severe ones.

The biggest cues for just about everybody are thoughts and conversations about cocaine, and I recommend that people avoid all these conversations. This includes talking about how terrible cocaine is for you, and how you are in treatment to help you get off. I recommend what I call the four-second conversation, which goes like this:

"I do not do cocaine anymore, so please don't offer me any." It takes five seconds to say, "I do not do cocaine anymore, so please don't offer me any. And I am not selling it anymore, either." This is a very important point, because people who want to quit cocaine can't deal it and expect not to use it at the same time. *You must avoid selling it as well as using it!* You literally can't handle it. These two things are equally important, so please do yourself a favor and stay away from all conversations about cocaine.

Also stay away from songs like "Cocaine," sung by Eric Clapton, which may remind you of the drug; news briefs about cocaine busts; movies like *Scarface,* which are about cocaine topics, and so on. For some people, drinking coffee or smoking cigarettes are cues because coffee or tobacco gives them a rush. Look carefully at your behavioral patterns in determining what your cues are.

Desensitization

activity #1

After making your list of cues, from mild to moderate to severe, the next step is to use your relaxation program and learn how to relax in response to all three kinds. Start with the mild cues and check your pulse. Put yourself in a relaxed situation so that your pulse gets very slow, and then think about one of the mild cues. If your pulse begins to increase, relax yourself and let your breathing slow down in order to reduce the pulse rate; then go back to thinking about the mild cue. In this way, you can work up to those cues that you have listed as severe, or high-risk, and relax consciously so that you won't be surprised by an exaggerated response when those cues come up in your everyday life.

This technique is called desensitization, and it has proved very useful over the years to people who have phobias. It is interesting to note that the phobic response, which is an anxiety response, is the same physiological response experienced in the urge to do cocaine. The cocaine urge is labeled as pleasurable, and the phobic or anxiety response as unpleasurable, but they have the same physiological sensations; it is only the label that is different—and we are the one who put the label on our feelings and responses. Again, we see that the mind is a very powerful tool that we ourselves can use to change our responses and relabel our feelings.

Let's return to the example of Josh. He learned to relax and not respond with a drug urge to cues such as the restaurants where he used to lunch with his friend. He still has high-pressure days much like those that set him up to do cocaine in the first place, but he has learned how to relax in response to those pressures and to deal with his busy days without having urges to do cocaine. His ability to function effectively throughout the day was increased.

The Behavioral Risk Scale (B.R.S.)

You can see that it is important, now that you are aware of behavioral cues, to stay away from high-risk situations. Parties and weddings are often situations to avoid during early recovery because so often they are places where people do a lot of cocaine. It is too much to expect in early recovery to set yourself up in situations where you have to constantly refuse to do cocaine, so be good to yourself and avoid them. It's important to be honest about these situations and not try to "white-knuckle" your way through a party or event that you know will be high-risk to you. Set yourself up with supports, and stay away from places you know are dangerous to your program of recovery. You are the one who makes the choice to go or not go. You are in control.

A good way to decide which situations are high-risk is to use the Behavioral Risk Scale, or B.R.S. Think about a scale of 1 through 10, with 1 being very low-risk for the presence of cocaine and 10 being those very high-risk situations where you know cocaine will be offered to you.

Anything above a 5 in terms of risk is simply unacceptable in early recovery. *Be good to yourself!* Stay below a 5 and take care of yourself by being very clear about which situations are high-risk for you. Identify those situations ahead of time, and remember: Any friends who aren't supporting your recovery aren't very good friends.

Keeping Track of Your Progress

At the end of each day, recognize the improvement that you have made. Notice how much your urges and thoughts about cocaine have decreased each day, and give yourself credit for this. Take it one day at a time. *Tell yourself that cocaine is something you used to do.* It is very important to think about your cocaine use in the past tense, and all the behaviors concerning cocaine as being things that occurred in the past.

Remember how powerful your thoughts are in setting up feeling states that can lead—or not lead—to an urge for the drug. Be kind to yourself and reinforce, in your mind, that you are doing well and treating yourself well and that cocaine is something you used to do. Reinforce these new healthy behaviors and this positive way of thinking whenever you think about yourself, and avoid negative thoughts about yourself to yourself, as these are destructive and can lead to relapses.

If you should relapse, or experiment to see if you can go back and try cocaine again, please don't beat yourself and call yourself a failure. Put the whip away. Don't give yourself a hard time with guilt and remorse, because if you do you will have trouble getting back on your program. Many people do cocaine because they think poorly of themselves, and this hopelessness leads to their using cocaine again and again. This will not help you. So take it one day at a time again, and go back to your program of relaxation and positive reinforcement. Many people have used this program to stay clean for a long time, one day at a time, and you can too. Give yourself credit for the time you have been clean and the progress you have made, and go back to taking care of yourself. Think about cocaine as something in your past, and don't destroy yourself with remorse.

7

Thirty Successful Strategies to Help You Get Off Cocaine and Stay Off

There are many strategies you can use to help yourself get off cocaine and stay off. Whether you decide to go into treatment or do it on your own, many of the same guidelines still apply. Some of these strategies were outlined in previous chapters of the book in greater detail, but this chapter brings them all together.

1. Limit conversations to four seconds. I am listing the four-second conversation as number one because it is *the* most important strategy that you have in your bag of tricks. This is because conversations about cocaine lead to thoughts about cocaine, and these thoughts are potentially very dangerous to your determination to get off and stay off. When I say "four-second conversation," I mean that you are literally allowed no more than four seconds to talk about cocaine. Say something like, "I do not do cocaine anymore, so please don't offer me any. I don't want to discuss it." Please take me very literally, because any more than four seconds is dangerous. You may add one more second, making it a five-second conversation, if you used to deal or smuggle, by adding, "And I do not deal anymore, either." Conversations about cocaine are the *biggest* reason for most people's failure to follow through on their decision to quit using.

2. Stay away from alcohol. I usually recommend that everyone in outpatient treatment drink no alcoholic beverages for at least three months in their early recovery. They must not drink until they are clean for at least three months, because alcohol is so closely associated with cocaine in most people's minds. It does not matter whether they used alcohol before or after the cocaine use, it only matters that *most people associate alcohol with cocaine* in their minds. One reason for this is that they are more likely to say yes than no to an offer of a line of cocaine after an alcoholic beverage, and this makes it a danger in and of itself. Many people are also conditioned to associate alcohol with coming down off of a cocaine high, and this is another reason why it is dangerous. Alcohol and cocaine go together like red beans and rice, as we used to say in New Orleans when I was in graduate school. They go hand in hand, and so this connection—or conditioning response, as a behavioral psychologist would call it—must be avoided at all costs. By no alcohol, I really mean *no alcohol:* no beer, no wine, no hard liquor. Also remember that alcohol is addictive for many people, and the last thing you need in your recovery is a different addiction.

3. Call your dealer. This is a very important strategy, but please do not undertake it alone. Have somebody with you who is not a cocaine user when you call your dealer, so that you won't get into trouble with this telephone call. Tell your dealer that you are not using anymore and you are not buying anymore. But that is *all* you need to say—you do not need to get into a conversation. Remember strategy number one, the four-second conversation, and follow it rigidly here. If the dealer has an answering machine, that's great; use it. Leave a message: "This is so-and-so; I don't use anymore and I do not want to hear from you." Again, have someone you trust who is a non-user there with you to support you on this call. If you are in treatment or therapy you could make the call from your counselor's office; if not, a good friend can certainly give support on this one. Calling the dealer is important because it is part of the commitment you are making to yourself to stay clean. Making this commitment involves an increase in self-respect, perhaps the first time you've respected yourself in a long time.

4. Tell your family. This is very important because so often members of your family know there is a problem but don't know what it is. They know something has been wrong for some time and things are just not adding up and something's very definitely on your mind, and they usually want to help. So don't be surprised if you open up and tell your family and they respond, "We knew there was something wrong." This is very common. One of the reasons we have families is to give and receive love and support, so please don't sell your family short. Let them support you. Nine times out of ten that's just what they want to do. Your family can also be a source of financial help if you need to go into treatment. We need our families more than ever at times like this.

5. Set up a financial work sheet. The financial work sheet is a very useful tool in recovery. Sit down with a piece of paper and pencil and add up the amount of money that you spent on cocaine over the past year, being *really honest* with yourself about it. Then add on another 30 to 50 percent more, because your estimate is probably much too conservative, and take a close look at your present financial situation. After you have a good idea of just how much money you have "invested" in cocaine use over the past year, write down something you want that you could have had with that money. This is instructive because it gives you a motive for getting well.

Be very clear about what it is that you could have spent that money on besides cocaine, because this is going to be the thing you will start saving for, now that you are not using and are free to save money. For example, I treated a patient who wanted to stop paying rent but who had spent $20,000 the previous year on cocaine, easily a down payment on a nice house. As soon as he understood that this was the case he began to save toward a real down payment, a realistic and important goal for his motivation.

Keep in mind that you did not get into this financial mess overnight, so on your work sheet include the amount of time it took for you to get into the financial straits you are currently in, including any bad credit, debts, trouble with checking accounts or bank cards, advance money accounts, etc. When you have added up the amount of money you owe, also add up the number of months it took you to get where you are and double that total to get an estimate of how long it will take you to get out of it. It will take you about twice as long to get out of debt as it did to get into it. Keep this work sheet and refer back to it throughout your first year of recovery. You will see an improvement financially, and this measurable comparison of progress and improvement will reinforce your determination.

People who become addicted to a substance often have little tolerance for frustration and are very short on patience. Therefore, it is important to give yourself rewards for the improvement you are making, even though you have not yet reached your goal. Also be clear on your work sheet about other smaller financial rewards you can give to yourself throughout this period while you are saving and rebuilding financially again. Even a little thing like buying a new pair of shoes or making some special effort about your appearance or giving yourself a small treat or recreation—anything that is a tangible reminder of financial improvement here—is worthwhile because it is an acknowledgment that you are choosing to spend your money this way when before the money would have gone for cocaine. Give yourself credit for your improvement and reinforce your self-esteem, not only by making it to your goals but by appreciating your progress along the way.

6. Use the dead-letter technique. A dead letter is one that is written but never mailed. I often have my patients write dead letters to the person or persons they least want to know about their cocaine use. These letters are usually never mailed, but they can be great motivators to get well because they help you face your situation honestly. A father, for instance, might write to his children about his cocaine use. It is the process of writing the letter that is most important, allowing you to examine honestly and privately your situation and helping you to work through your grief process.

7. Write a contingency contract. Contingency contracts can be used in tandem with dead letters if you like. A contingency contract is an agreement that you will tell someone about your cocaine use whom you really don't want to know about it as a kind of consequence if you should go back to using cocaine. Some physicians, lawyers, and nurses have used contingency contracting to help them stay clean by agreeing to send a letter to the appropriate authorities about their cocaine use should they fall back into using again. The letter would be a dead letter and never mailed if the person stays clean; if not, the letter would be mailed as a consequence of the relapse. Your therapist might agree to keep a copy of the letter, or you may want to keep the letter yourself or make an agreement with a friend or family member to mail it for you should you slip.

8. Change regular patterns. It's helpful to change some patterns you have in your life in order to break up any old habits that are associated with cocaine use or are an excuse for cocaine use. For instance, if you take a certain route home from work, past your dealer's house, find a different way. If you have a pattern of staying home and isolating yourself that you associate with your cocaine use, find ways to get out and be around people who are clean and are low-risk company for you. It is important that you identify your patterns, especially the dangerous ones that are associated with cocaine use, so you can change them and reduce your risk of using. Even little things like the route you take home from work every day can be a constant reminder and acknowledgment to yourself that you are changing many things about yourself and looking at things in a whole different way. It also encourages you to see that you have some control over your life and the events that happen to you, and this is a very positive understanding.

9. Change your environment. You can change your environment in many ways, creating new routines and new viewpoints for yourself. An inpatient hospital program or residential program breaks up old patterns and gives you new people to interact with, but this is only one option. If you used to use at home in an isolated situation on the weekend, make plans for social weekends away from home. If you went to a particular place to use, such as a bar or a friend's house, change that habit to one you do not associate with cocaine use.

10. Entertain at home. This is an important strategy, because when we entertain at home we have more control than we do when we go to someone else's house. That is to say, we make the rules in our own homes and we can be more comfortable saying "Please don't come over if you have cocaine" or "Please don't come over when you are loaded, I do not use cocaine anymore." Most people would be uncomfortable saying that at someone else's place, and it is often easier to invite friends to our home or meet them in a neutral place like a restaurant where we have more control over the environment. Be very clear with yourself and your friends about visiting in homes where you know it is likely that cocaine will be present. You don't need to put yourself under that kind of stress.

11. Follow a solid nutritional program. A nutritional program was outlined in chapter 4 under "Cocaine and Nutrition." It is important to keep your physical and mental states stable. Anything that upsets your stability puts you at risk for an urge to use cocaine, so follow your nutritional and vitamin supplement program carefully and regularly.

12. Open up. Part of the drug addiction process involves closing down with regard to other people and covering up about your drug use and about changes in your life and what you're really feeling. Opening up to people and becoming less isolated is part of the healing process and is critical to successful treatment and recovery, so begin to open up and let those who care about you know what's really going on. You will find that the people who are really your friends and who really love you will appreciate this and feel closer to you, and this is important because you need the support of your friends right now.

13. Use the PRE technique. The PRE technique was outlined in chapter 5. I cannot emphasize the value of this technique enough; I believe it is responsible for 70 percent of the recoveries in outpatient programs. You do not need a therapist to teach you the technique. All you need to do is follow the description in this book. It works!

14. Move, if necessary. Many people do not need to change their residences or their jobs, although sometimes it is warranted. If you were a dealer or smuggler it may be very important, or if you have been living with a dealer or a heavy user. It is almost impossible to stay clean if you are living in a situation where cocaine is present at all times, so move if you need to. Set up your working and living situations to support staying clean, and don't subject yourself to the constant stress of living or working where cocaine is always available.

15. Screen communications. The most common example of a communications problem involves telephones and answering machines, because so often connections are made on the phone. You may want to change your telephone number and install an answering machine because this allows you to screen your calls and gives you control over which calls you respond to. Don't be at the whim of other people calling in; stay in control of your communications. You may even need to get an unlisted telephone number if you were a dealer, or if your dealing and using friends are very persistent.

16. Assert yourself. This is very important in early recovery because you may have forgotten how to say no.

General assertiveness techniques, such as the "broken record" technique, may be helpful at this time. To use this technique, just repeat that you do not use cocaine and do not want to discuss it, over and over if you must, because some people will test you. These may be people that you care about very much, but if they keep offering you cocaine or bringing up the topic for discussion, you will simply need to assert yourself: "No, I don't talk about that and I don't use it anymore." If necessary, hang up on them or walk away, as many times as is needed for them to understand that you are serious.

17. Use the Cocaine Hotline. This is a very important resource for support in early recovery, especially if you are not in therapy and are handling your own treatment on a self-help basis. The 800-COCAINE number operates free on a 24-hour-a-day basis, and whether you are in a crisis situation or just need some support, dial it. There will be someone at the other end of the line to talk to you who has been through it too. If you need referrals for therapy, they can be provided as well. These people are there to help you and to offer support, so use them!

18. Join Cocaine Anonymous (C.A.). Cocaine Anonymous is a free self-help group available in many areas of the country. You can find a local meeting by calling the national office in Los Angeles, which is listed under Cocaine Anonymous, at 1-213-839-1141, Culver City. This is a wonderful source of support, because the group members meet regularly and have one goal in common—to stay off cocaine. Get all the support you can at this time; there is no reason to do everything on your own when support is available.

19. Hibernate. Often early recovery is a time of hibernation because your social life was so involved with cocaine that you have few clean friends. Accept this if it is the case and lie low socially for a while until you can make new friends who are non-users. One of the advantages of groups like Cocaine Anonymous is that it is a way to meet new friends who are committed to staying clean. But if you have to go into a period of hibernation for a while, just accept this as part of early recovery. It won't last forever.

20. Work on grief and loss issues. You can often identify issues involved with loss and grief on your own. The importance of this is that people who started using cocaine heavily at the time of a loss or grief in their lives can begin, in early recovery, to identify the incomplete grief processes and take steps to complete them. If you used cocaine as a way of dealing with loss in order to anesthetize the pain, remember that *the pain and the sadness will not kill you but the cocaine could.* Learn to deal with sadness, knowing that it is a process and will not last forever.

21. Stop dealing. This may seem obvious, but it is very important. If you have a history of dealing cocaine, you must stop, because it is virtually impossible to stop using while you are still dealing. This is also true for smuggling operations; it is impossible to stop using when you are still smuggling or acting as a runner or contact for drug connections.

22. Use the Behavioral Risk Scale (B.R.S.). The Behavioral Risk Scale, described in the last chapter, is a scale from 1 to 10 of how risky certain people, places, or things are to you. On the scale, 1 is no risk, 10 is relapse, and any risk above a 5 is too great. In other words, consider where a person, place, thing, or event falls on the scale in your mind, and if it is a 5 or above, your risk of using cocaine is too great. You need to change the situation to reduce the risk. For example, I had a patient who was about to be married and his buddies were throwing a bachelor party for him. He used the Behavioral Risk Scale and determined that the bachelor party put him at about a 10 in terms of risk, and that that was unacceptably high. I made some suggestions to him to reduce his level of risk to not over a 5, one of which was to call the fellow who was organizing the bachelor party and tell him that he wasn't using and didn't want anybody to bring cocaine or come loaded. Another was that he should not drink any alcohol at the party. With these two suggestions, the risk of the party was decreased to about a 5, which he found acceptable. He attended the bachelor party, had a good time, and did not use cocaine. This made him very happy.

This is a good example of using the Behavioral Risk Scale as a mental tool to judge situations. One of the benefits of using the scale is that it gives you a couple of minutes to consider the situation, and those few minutes are in and of themselves risk-reducing, because you are thinking about the situation and structuring it ahead of time to reduce the risk of using. So buy some time for yourself by using the Behavioral Risk Scale.

23. Let your friends know you are quitting. If your friends are real friends, they will support you in your decision, so let them know that you are not using cocaine anymore, don't want to talk about it, and don't want them around you when they are loaded. They need to know the rules for being around you as you get off and stay off cocaine. So give your friends a chance to support you and show that they are real friends. If they do not support you, or if they try to sabotage you, they are not your friends and should be dropped.

24. Stop "stinking thinking." "Stinking thinking" is a phrase used in Alcoholics Anonymous to describe any kind of thinking that will eventually lead to using drugs or alcohol. A good example of this kind of thinking might be going back to your dealer to pay a debt. This leads to using cocaine, because once you get to the dealer you don't just pay the debt, all too often you end up incurring a new one by buying cocaine and using it. If you owe a debt to a dealer, pay it indirectly by mailing the money or having it delivered by a third party. Any kind of thinking that leads you into a high-risk situation on the Behavioral Risk Scale is stinking thinking and should be avoided at all costs.

25. Identify your cues. Chapter 6 talks a lot about cues or triggers for cocaine use. It is important to identify these cues, because only in this way will you be able to avoid them. I call this "cue reduction"—avoiding whatever triggers the urge to use cocaine.

26. *Get rid of paraphernalia.* Any scales, jars, pipes—*anything* you have used in connection with cocaine—must be gotten rid of. Even storage areas where you have kept cocaine should be rearranged. You may want to redecorate one or more rooms that you associate with cocaine use. Remember, the more intimately associated the place or thing is with cocaine, the more important it is to get rid of it. As I have said, move if you must.

27. *Find support systems.* Identify and rally whatever support systems you have, and bring in the human beings who care about you. You need all the support you can get. You should have a telephone list of people you know and trust, who are clean, whom you can call should you feel an urge to use cocaine.

28. *Stop carrying cash.* Cash in your pocket or purse is often a cue for a cocaine purchase, so keep your available cash to $25 or less. Have your paycheck deposited directly to your bank, if possible, or ask someone you trust to accept the cash if that is the way you are usually paid.

29. *Get rid of credit cards and bank withdrawal cards.* Never carry anything with you that will make it easy for you to purchase cocaine. The so-called "cash cards" that allow you to get money from automatic teller machines are a particular temptation in early recovery. If you don't trust yourself, ask someone you do trust to help you with your finances while you find your balance in early recovery.

30. *Do a values inventory.* This is a time when you can take stock of who you are as a person by clarifying what your priorities are. In making a values inventory, first identify the values you were raised with, the things taught to you by your parents. Then identify the values you are currently living by. Then go on to identify which values you wish to keep and which ones you wish to change. This will help you identify what your three highest priorities are, the ones that you are unwilling to compromise on. Getting your values straight helps you to get your purpose in life straight, and when you know your purpose in life you will be able to identify goals and accomplish them. This will help you to stay clean and on track to where you choose to go.

If you carefully follow these recommendations to get off and stay off cocaine, you are assured of success. So follow them carefully and consistently, and accept my congratulations, for you are joining the ranks of thousands of people who are getting off cocaine and staying off.

8

Families and Cocaine

Cocaine use can have a very serious effect on the stability of a family. Use by the parents is most common, with accompanying damage to the family economically and emotionally, but families increasingly are having to deal with cocaine addiction in a teenage son or daughter. Cocaine abuse is a jealous lover, and the family member involved with it often has no time or energy—or money—left for family activities.

John, the contractor I described earlier, was locked out of the house by his wife, who was completely fed up with his behavior. She left this letter pinned to the door for him to read:

John,

I don't know where you have been or why. I called Lou's house and found out that you left there about 9:15. Why can't you come home? I'm writing this letter because you are never here for me to talk to. You work all the time and still we have no money. I don't believe getting well is your first concern. You promised me you would do something every night and yet you didn't, even though you knew you might need to go to the hospital. I just wish you were more committed to staying clean.

What am I to do? I refuse to sit home one more night alone and wonder where you are, who you are with, and what you are doing. I think that it is my fault that you don't stay clean, and I wish that you were more committed to

*this. What am I to do? I think it's my fault that you don't take
me seriously. The boys don't either. I tell them—stop or else
you will get into trouble, and they don't stop because they
know that I am not going to follow through. Well, I have
threatened you so many times that you don't believe me
either. It is all very sad. I have been praying a lot, and the
only answer I can come up with is that I need to be by
myself and to be in charge of my own life and my children.*

*Our family life is crazy! It goes in spurts of normal–
abnormal. I need to just have it be normal all the time. You
don't follow through on anything to do with getting well.
Books go unread, appointments are missed, no vitamins,
no exercise, no tapes. Your life makes no sense. I am so
angry with you! When are you going to stop ruining
everything? Your word means nothing to me. How can we
build our marriage?*

*If you are ready to make a commitment, then it is time for
you to be on your own. I can no longer help you. When you
don't come home, I get physically ill. Please leave me
alone. When you can honestly say that you are well, then I
can look at you again.*

*I've tried to be your friend and your partner, and you fight
me on every mission. You keep pushing me away—I don't
know if I can sleep now. I just know that I cannot stay on
this roller coaster any longer—enough is enough.*

                                                                Doris

John read this letter aloud a number of times in group
therapy meetings. Every time he read it, he cried. I think
this letter says it all when it comes to families and cocaine
addiction: the sadness, the desperation, the aloneness
that the wife feels, and the helplessness. Spouses who
do not use cocaine often feel that it is somehow their fault
that their husband or wife is addicted to a substance.
They take the blame and feel and behave very much like
martyrs, and when the using spouse has a relapse, the
non-using spouse will take the blame for that too, saying,
"Well, it's really my fault because I was angry," or, "I
complained to him the other day about some things that
were going wrong in the family."

Family Support

Please remember that if you are a non-using spouse—
or "co-addict," as we call it—it is *not your fault* that your
partner uses a substance addictively. You are not to
blame. Addiction is a disease that affects the whole family, and part of the recovery process for the addict includes other family members taking responsibility for their
actions only and understanding that the addict is responsible for his or her acts. You are not responsible for each
other's behavior, on this or any other occasion.

It is very important for non-using family members to
become active in support groups like Narc-Anon or Al-
Anon, the family support group attached to Alcoholics
Anonymous, because contacts with other families going
through the same thing will help you to understand that
you can love the person who is addicted while at the
same time detaching yourself from the addictive behavior.
You can work on achieving this even if your spouse or
child is still using the drug. It can change your attitude
toward living in a home with an addicted family member.
Narc-Anon or Al-Anon members can help you understand
that acting as if you are in some way the cause of the
problem makes the problem worse, because this as-
sumes that family members have control over the behavior of the spouse or child, and *you do not.* So get help for
the family even if the addict is not ready to get treatment.
You will receive some needed support for yourself and
learn some strategies that may be helpful in getting the
using spouse in for help sooner.

Some of the strategies that are helpful in getting a
using spouse or child into treatment are also painful. For
instance, the letter that you read earlier in this chapter
was written as a result of a recommendation I made to
John's wife that she actually lock her husband out of the
house and leave a note explaining her actions. I suggested this to help her see that she could love her husband and yet not support the addictive behavior that was

so destructive to their family life. Her husband was stealing money from the family at this time, and the rent was
unpaid, and she didn't know where they were going to be
living the next month. She didn't even know if she would
have money to buy groceries for her boys for the following
week. With things so desperate at home, a fairly radical
move had to be made to change the situation. Because
of the letter, John stayed out for two days on a binge, but
eventually he came back and checked himself into the
hospital for a thirty-day treatment program, which was
exactly what he needed. I am making no guarantees; this
type of action does not always work. But putting pressure
on using individuals, so that they feel the consequences
of what they are doing, often helps to get them into treatment sooner. Families should feel that seeking treatment
themselves, even if the using spouse is not ready to do
this, can be productive. Strategies and help in implement-
ing them are available.

Family Interventions

The second kind of intervention that can be helpful for
families involves family intervention meetings. This technique has been developed over the last fifteen years in
treating alcoholics, and it is also useful for cocaine addicts. Again, the goal is to help get abusers into treatment
before they ruin their lives or perhaps kill themselves as
a result of their addiction. Because the consequences of
addiction are so serious, radical moves must sometimes
be made.

Family interventions can take place in a therapist's
office or in the family's home. The process involves several meetings with the family, designed to help the using
family member understand some of the consequences
and pain involved in the habit, pain that is involved for the
family as well as for the user. These meetings can also
include neighbors or employers or anyone else who is

involved in the addict's abuse and who can, perhaps, have a positive effect.

The purpose of the meeting with the using family member is to point out in a caring way that the behaviors being exhibited are causing problems to other people and problems in the user's own life. This lets using family members know that they are loved and cared about and that others are noticing that their life is going downhill. Those involved must emphasize that they want to help stop this process before it is too late.

This type of family intervention is effective about 80 percent of the time for getting using family members into treatment, and you should consider it if you are in a situation where it might be of help. You can set up the process by calling a treatment center and asking for help from a family intervention specialist or by calling a therapist in private practice who is trained in doing family interventions.

Often having children involved in therapy sessions or interventions is very effective. The children can state in a simple and direct way some of the problems caused by the using family member, and this can be very powerful. This experience also affords the children a way to express some of their feelings. Children know that something is going on when there are problems at home. They pick up the tension level in the family even if the situation itself isn't discussed or explained to them. It will often reassure them to understand what is happening and to know that they can have a role in helping a parent or an older brother or sister get into treatment. Children often mirror the sense of helplessness that the non-using spouse feels, so involving them in Al-Anon or Narc-Anon and the intervention process can help give them a sense of belonging to a family, a sense they may have lost during the time when the family was so disrupted by drug use.

There is help and hope for the family, including the children, even if intervention doesn't work to get the using member into treatment. Don't give up; go to support meetings or go into therapy individually to get help on how to handle your own life. It is important that we use methods and techniques that have been used in alcohol abuse treatment, for instance, and apply them where appropriate in working with the families of cocaine addicts. These techniques are very powerful in helping not only the using member but the whole family, and they are often very useful in getting people into treatment.

9

Couples and Cocaine

There are several variations that occur when cocaine is involved in a couple's relationship. Both members may be using cocaine more or less heavily, and it can become a real problem in the relationship. Or one partner may be a user with a problem while the other does not use cocaine at all. Or one partner may have a cocaine problem while the other has stopped using cocaine but is still trying to continue with the relationship. Each possibility is different, but there are interventions that may help with each.

The Intimacy Circle

All three variations on couples relationships can use the exercise that I call the Intimacy Circle, which consists of having each partner draw two circles, one representing the self and the other the partner, in relationship. It is interesting to see how much overlap, if any, exists between the two circles. In relationships where there is mutual drug dependence, one circle may be right on top of the other, with almost complete overlap. This is a very powerful statement about a relationship; the people in this situation have very little autonomy and are extremely dependent upon each other and the drug. The only kind of relationship that can tolerate a complete overlap dependency successfully is mother and fetus, and even then the mother needs her thoughts and feelings to be her own. All normal adult individuals need space to breathe.

In a healthy relationship there is considerable overlap of the two circles but some areas of independent action as well. In relationships where the two circles are so separate that they are hardly touching one another, the couple is probably separating or divorcing. Of course the partners may also have very different perceptions of the balance, and this causes conflicts because of the threat of too little or—often perceived by the woman—too much autonomy. Understanding the tensions and imbalances inherent in all relationships may be another of the gifts of recovery from drug addiction, allowing the couple either to become stronger in their relationship or to disengage and find happiness in very different lives. A woman who expects to be taken care of entirely or a man who believes he must control every detail of his relationship can learn the critical balance of independence and vulnerability that underlie all healthy relationships.

The first kind of relationship is where both partners are using cocaine. Marium is an example. She got involved with using cocaine when she was living with a man who was both a user and a dealer. Marium came to the conclusion, as many people do when they quit cocaine, that she must separate from her partner if he continued to use, and she eventually left the relationship. This was a very painful decision. With a couple where there is mutual drug use, there is a dependency relationship. In other words, we are not talking about two adults living together; the relationship is more like that of two children. This may work out satisfactorily while cocaine is available, but when either the money or the drug runs out, the fact that someone has to play parent and either supply more drugs or set limits on the drug use, saying, "This has gone too far, let's quit now," presents a problem. There is often a period of pause in the relationship while both partners wait to see whether or not the roles will change and one of them will go from being a child to being the parent. These relationships have the best chance of success when both partners go into treatment together, because stopping the use of cocaine involves a radical change in roles and an adjustment for both partners. Marium discovered that she had to go from being dependent to being an adult alone. Her partner wanted to continue with his pattern of use and his past role within the relationship, so she left him. Sometimes this radical action will bring the other partner into counseling, but whether it does or not, walking out of the relationship and into a drug-free life is worth it for the partner who can do it, painful as it is.

The second kind of relationship is where one person uses cocaine and the other does not, and the third is where one partner is using and the other partner has stopped. Although there are important insights available to a partner who has used cocaine before but has quit, these two are very similar for the purpose of counseling, so I will discuss them together. In this situation, one partner does become like the parent. Usually the non-using spouse takes on the parental role, and the one who is still using takes on the child role. This is a very stressful situation in a relationship because the punishing parent/bad child connection is not healthy for adults. As you might guess, this couple will also often have sexual problems, complicated by the cocaine use and the parental attitude, that go deep into their everyday life as well.

The partner playing the role of the bad child feels guilty and uses that guilt to excuse using cocaine again. Guilt is a very destructive dynamic for these individuals; I often call it self-rape. Guilt has absolutely no productive function in adult human beings. It is merely a way in which we beat ourselves up and make ourselves feel badly enough to justify using drugs again to get a temporary lift. Obviously, guilt needs to be recognized and avoided in order to stop this vicious cycle.

When I work with couples, I remind them to try to

decrease both the guilt and the blaming that feed this cycle. We work on realigning the roles within the relationship so that they are not one critical parent and one bad child, they are two adult people. It is important that they learn to have fun again, and even act like children at times, without the use of drugs. When they became more and more involved in the drug-use cycle, they may have forgotten the positive personality traits and qualities that drew them together in the first place. This is the time for couples with children to get a babysitter and allow themselves some time away to find some enjoyable non-goal-oriented activities to share. It is a time for rediscovering the positive things about their relationship, because without this rediscovery and role alignment, staying clean and staying together become very difficult tasks indeed.

The Marital Tune-Up

Another exercise I use is the Marital Tune-Up. This involves three key issues in a relationship—trust, power, and intimacy—and is an inventory of where the couple stands in terms of these issues. All three issues need to be examined, and realignments made, for the couple to function in a healthy way in early recovery. And of course it's a useful exercise for any couple, even one without drug problems.

Trust is the most important issue, because it is usually trust that suffers most when a partner becomes addicted. Trust cannot be built without faith, and no one can give us faith. Only we know whether we believe in the continuing existence of a relationship, and so I ask both partners whether they have this faith. If they both answer no in all honesty, then we talk about faith in depth and about some of the other options, including realigning, changing, or even terminating the relationship.

If they both do have faith in the continued existence of their relationship, we go on to talk about trust as something that can be built, a set of skills. Trust involves consistency between what people say they are going to do and what they actually do, and if each partner can believe that the other will do what he or she has said, the couple is building trust. If there is no consistency, trust suffers. In the relationship of a couple where one member is addicted, there is much inconsistency, and this needs to be worked on immediately. As John's wife, Doris, noted, she had trouble following through also, because she would threaten actions she wouldn't carry out. No one is perfect; we are all human, and 100 percent trust is too much to expect when two people live together. Something closer to 80 percent is more realistic, but both partners need to know that in most cases they can believe each other implicitly.

The next issue is power, and the power dynamic is often in need of realignment when these couples come in for counseling. These trust-power-intimacy dynamics are present, of course, for most couples in counseling, and, as I said earlier, I am simply applying known concepts to the early recovery process. Often one person has the overt or obvious power in a relationship and the other has covert or undercover—less obvious—power. For example, let's consider John and Doris. He had economic power in the relationship because he was the breadwinner and Doris stayed home with the kids. Doris did, however, have covert emotional power, as women often do. She exercised this power by being the one who was more in touch with her feelings and more able to express them; this is usually the woman's role in a relationship. (In gay relationships also, one partner is usually more in touch with feelings and so has the emotional power, while the other partner has the economic power.) Doris would get very upset with John because of his binges, and she would express anger toward him by withholding sex, another common behavior pattern for women. This is a powerful weapon and it was very disturbing for John, who was not only less in touch with his feelings but often confused about what sex had to do with other conflicts.

Doris was not aware of the fact that she was exercising covert power, but she learned to acknowledge this in a therapy situation. She and John both understood that this was very real power. John had been using his frustration and confusion as an excuse to use cocaine, and because Doris was what we call a co-addict, her pattern was to feel responsible for his use. She took the blame for behavior, in other words, that was his and not hers. Although this dynamic was involved in his drug use, she was *not* responsible for that use and needed to be reminded of this often in therapy as part of her early recovery. And John needed to be reminded that his behavior had consequences and was not a result of his wife's actions. His cocaine use was by his own choice.

The third dynamic is intimacy, and intimacy is very difficult to achieve in a relationship where there is little or no trust. This is because most women need to trust their partner before they are comfortable letting go sexually and responding on the physical level. Almost inevitably, couples coming in for counseling in the early stages of recovery from cocaine addiction are experiencing some sexual difficulties. This is also part of the reason why women who are non-using partners are reluctant to get involved sexually with their husband or lover, because the trust between them is so low they do not feel comfortable letting down the walls between them. Intimacy is often a problem for the partner who is using cocaine, too; Claudia Black's book *It'll Never Happen to Me,* about the adult children of alcoholics, describes how the anxiety-provoking subject of intimacy is handled by people with this history. As I pointed out in chapter 3, many cocaine addicts are children of at least one alcoholic or susbtance-abusing parent, and they may have learned at an early age to protect themselves against parental inconsistency. Because they could never predict how their parent or parents would behave emotionally, they learned that it is safer not to be intimate or close to other human beings because they can be embarrassed and hurt so easily.

These fears, which seem quite reasonable based on the experiences of the partners, must be brought out and worked on if the treatment is to be successful.

The first order of business is to acknowledge these fears, and the second is to begin to understand them by reading or by attending support group meetings, such as the special Al-Anon meetings for adult children of alcoholics. People are complex and are often living situations that go back to their childhood without recognizing that their responses form a pattern that is not satisfactory even to themselves. A cocaine addict may need Alcoholics Anonymous to help with the addiction—but may also be able to use information found in co-addict groups to understand the addiction of a parent or current partner.

Another reason why intimacy is such a big issue is that people who become addicted to cocaine are often very goal- and achievement-oriented. These goals and achievements are external. Josh, for instance, was very achievement-oriented in an economic sense. He earned over $200,000 a year and also came into a large inheritance, most of which he spent on cocaine. But like many people who become involved in cocaine, he forgot that there is a difference between purpose in life and external goals. It is important, as part of the values inventory I mentioned earlier, that you start out delineating your purpose in life, your larger purpose, and that you ask yourself, "Why am I here on this earth?" If you are very clear on your purpose, your goals will fall into place, but if you are not clear, you may focus only on external goals, such as money and prestige, and get into a lot of trouble. Money and prestige are wonderful things, but they are *not substitutes for love and affection!* They are not interchangeable. Love and affection are essentials for any human being, and when they are not present in your life you will feel an emptiness and lack of purpose that can be dangerous, leading to aimlessness and self-destructive behavior.

This is what happened to Josh, but in early recovery

he regained a sense of purpose. For him, this was to represent his clients in his law practice ethically and truthfully, and to be of some service to people who could not afford an expensive lawyer. Giving service to others had meaning for him. This often becomes important in early recovery, whether from cocaine or other addictions. Patients begin to see beyond themselves to a larger purpose in their lives. Acting on this purpose is very satisfying and leads to a sense of serenity. Josh attained that sense of serenity, and with it came the love and affection he had always wanted. He finally realized that no amount of achievement and recognition could substitute for love, and he set his shorter-range goals to be consistent with his larger purpose. He was no longer fragmented and aimless.

It is important for couples to share their individual purposes, for if they have different aims in their lives, it will be difficult for them to work together as a couple. Conflicts are inevitable in a relationship when purposes are in conflict.

Inventory of Rapport Levels

The next step in working with a couple is to begin to identify their level of rapport on the four planes of existence: physical, mental, emotional, and spiritual. This is a kind of inventory as well. At first, each partner needs to get in touch with where he or she is on these four planes, as outlined in chapter 4. Then the couple goes through this process together, sharing with each other to see if there is a blending or at least a complementarity on these levels. Couples often have one or two levels where they have difficulties with this rapport.

For example, in making their inventory, John and Doris came to the conclusion that they had a very good mental level of rapport and a very good spiritual level, but physically and emotionally they were very different. Some of Doris's needs for emotional support were brought out, and John began to understand that there were things he could do to help Doris feel more secure emotionally. At the physical level, Doris began to realize that John needed a lot more physical touching and reassurance, some in the form of sexual contact and some not. Doris's tendency in the past had been to assume that every time John touched her he was asking for intimate sexual contact. This was not so. They began to work on this together, and both began to feel more comfortable and accepting with each other on a physical level, learning how to share physical affection without assuming that there was a goal or an end to the contact that was sexual. The contact in and of itself felt very good and did not need to have a goal to be pleasurable. Many people who are recovering from cocaine addiction need to realize that relationships do not necessarily have to have goals. Relationships, by their very nature, are process-oriented, and it is important to focus on the present and on receiving and giving pleasure now.

Although women are more likely to stay with men through addiction and recovery than men are with women, I watched Doris stay with John through many situations in which most wives would have left their husbands. Part of the reason she stayed was because she worked with the Al-Anon program and had family counseling. She was able to recover from her own co-addictive illness and realize that she was not responsible for his addiction. This kept her sane through a lot of difficult situations. The love she felt for John was a beautiful thing, and it sustained her through many difficult times. But it is the knowledge and wisdom that she received from other families' support that helped her realize that she could continue to love John while detaching herself from his addictive behavior.

10

Women
and Cocaine

I am including two chapters in this book that are specialized by sex because I believe there are some areas of difference between men and women in their use of cocaine. As a matter of fact, I believe that, although men and women are equal, there are important cultural and physical differences between them; and if men and women are different, it is important to recognize those differences in treatment approach.

In the study done by the 800-COCAINE hotline, Dr. Gold says they found this description of women (p. 12):

> When looked at separately, the experience of the women on cocaine was much like that of the men. They, too, were well educated, earned relatively high incomes, had used the drug for an average of four years, had binged, and reported suffering the same problems as men. A similar proportion had tried to commit suicide. We conclude, as have others, that as women become better educated, suffer the same stresses as men in connection with their careers, earn substantial salaries, and live similar lifestyles, they, too, seek "to be with it," to be part of the crowd, to do what's trendy. Often, this means abusing the same substances—alcohol, cigarettes, or drugs—with the same sorry results.

And Bonnie-Jean Kimball in her study of women alcoholics notes a problem that is also true for women who abuse cocaine: "Denial of the illness is rampant in our

society. We have no methods of prevention or intervention that are as strong or as sophisticated as the ways in
which a woman and those around her deny her drug
dependence."

Women are usually more concerned with the emotional
aspects of a relationship than men are, and for this reason
they often stay with partners who have an addictive problem, while men in similar situations tend to leave. Many
if not most women with cocaine problems got involved
with the drug originally when it was offered to them by a
boyfriend or husband. One woman said, "I wanted to get
close to him. I would have eaten ice cream if that had
been offered instead." Ironically, a woman's cocaine use
often results in many more difficulties, not only with her
husband or boyfriend but with family and friends as well.
The triangle of man, woman, and cocaine is at least as
damaging to most relationships as a triangle with a third
person would be. Woman's place in a relationship, as I
noted in the last chapter, is often to be the keeper of the
emotional balance, and whether a woman uses cocaine
or not, if she is in a cocaine-influenced relationship, she
needs help.

Another important difference is that women are more
likely to open up to each other; that is to say, women are
more open about their feelings in women-only groups.
These groups can be a tremendous aid in treatment.
Some women find for the first time in their lives what it is
like to have a real friend. Many women have made the
man in their life their only friend. In recovery they learn
that this extreme dependence is neither healthy nor
necessary.

Another way women are different, as I mentioned earlier, has to do with trust in a sexual relationship. Women
have frequently reported that if they use cocaine more
and more often, they feel a barrier or wall between themselves and their partner, and this wall makes it very difficult to find sexual satisfaction. Another result of frequent
cocaine use in sexual connections is that the woman

involved begins to feel that there is something wrong with her sexually or the drug wouldn't be necessary. The most effective treatment for these problems is abstinence from cocaine. Most problems correct themselves over time, once the woman is clean. Some education in the effects of cocaine on sexuality is also very helpful. Part of the recovery process involves a reassessment of personal needs and needs within relationships, and an understanding of how women get caught up in relationships they don't feel good about.

For example, Marium had been living with a cocaine dealer for some time, and she was not comfortable either with the relationship or with her life-style. She said and did things she didn't feel good about. In therapy, she had to reassess, for herself, what she wanted out of her life and her relationship. Part of her reassessment had to do with the establishment of a purpose for her life, a topic we discussed in chapter 9, but she was also living in tremendous fear. We have seen that this is not unusual for those who develop a heavy cocaine habit. Some of the paranoia arises from the fact that the mind misperceives things as a result of cocaine use. Things that are normal stimuli become fear-evoking and the basis for paranoid delusions. Marium lived with this fear, and part of it was the feeling that she might be losing her mind. She consulted a psychiatrist but did not report her cocaine addiction. She was institutionalized for several days in a psychiatric facility, not in a substance abuse program but in a traditional locked psychiatric ward. Because she had been incarcerated against her will, it took some time for Marium to feel enough trust to seek out a new doctor. This time she was very careful to choose someone who was trained in the treatment of addictions.

I would like to quote from a letter she wrote at the time all this was happening in her life:

Dear Joan,
I have been thinking about writing this letter for a few days. Just couldn't get my thoughts together, but finally

decided to write and let the words simply come out as they will.

For a long time I have really kept two very separate lives within my life. My acting was pretty good, too. Now it seems difficult to continue this farce as I can no longer give a good performance anyway, except to average strangers. I also used to think that my activities and behavior didn't really interest anyone. I   aintained a high level of secrecy and only hinted at the type of life I was leading. During my year at [a facility where she worked as a teacher] and continuing up to the present, things have gotten progressively out of control. It seems like I stepped out of the shadows and people began to notice me and my behavior more and more.

You know how morbid and desperate I can get at times. And you can see that I react to my problems and fears by internalizing them and hurting myself. I punish myself so frequently that it is now the dominating activity in my life. I am unable to keep up a believable front, because I have lost or am losing my credibility and respect. I can't keep promises very well. I can't get the work I need to do accomplished on time; I am a topic for gossip, exaggeration, and pity. I say this without unrealistic paranoia. I am fooling no one with half a brain and eyes in their head.

I have many strengths. I have experience in education, talent, and intuition. But I don't use them. I let myself be controlled continually by fear and anxiety. I don't even make a pretense of disguising my actions or rationalizing my lies. There is no point to it anymore.

I also think that my problems go farther than my chronic drug abuse. My dreams, fantasies, art, and hallucinations are not new. I can't think about the future. I don't feel that I really have one. The only real thing in my life, what I live for, is my family. I wonder if that is enough? Maybe I should be getting more help, but I am really afraid of being institutionalized again. What can I do? Joan, I am destroying myself daily. I cannot romanticize it, and I can't live like this any longer. It is more and more difficult for me to function, and I am retreating into my own world—my private world, where no one else may enter, where I can be alone and

*forget who I am. Nobody to answer to, perform for; no one
will lie to me or try to analyze my life. I know it sounds like I
don't want to face life; I agree somewhat. I just don't want
to face horror, deceit, and [word unclear]. Most of the time
I spend trying to stay away from people. I get high, I work, I
write constantly, but my days are vague and without
purpose. I don't know where I'm heading.*

    *Going away was a distraction, it had its benefits, but
where are they now? When I'm working I try to be as careful
and comprehensive as possible, but I have very little of my
heart in it. It just seems to pass the time. It creates a whole
new crop of anxieties and inadequacies.*

At this point, Marium stopped the letter and switched
instead to writing her will. She brought it, a kind of free-
form will in very shaky handwriting, when she came for
her first therapy session. She was so concerned that she
might continue to want to purchase cocaine that she left
her home on the East Coast and came out to the West
Coast for therapy for a couple of months. She was afraid
of being institutionalized again and wanted to get away
from her family and her psychiatrist, in whom she had
minimal trust at the time. The isolation that she talks
about in the letter is common to all people who have an
addiction problem, and it becomes a progressive part of
the illness. It is not unusual for people to tell me stories
about how they isolated themselves in their homes with
a gun or a baseball bat, afraid that someone would come
to the door and try to harm them. Or for them to isolate
themselves in hotel rooms for days, living with visions
and sounds they were not even sure really existed, as it
is difficult, when high on cocaine, to know what exists
only in the mind. They live in a confusing world, like
something out of a surreal painting.

During the recovery process, Marium discovered some
things about herself that I'm going to share, because they
are important in the recovery process. One of the key
issues in cocaine addiction is that the cocaine use repre-
sents a message from the user to his or her world, or to

certain people in that world. For Marium, the message was that she was not getting what she wanted from her relationship, and she was in a state of sadness and depression. Another message had to do with her artwork and creativity. Like a lot of people who get involved with cocaine, Marium was a very achievement-oriented person, and while she was successful in business, the satisfaction only went so far. She liked earning a lot of money but felt that she had to deny the part of herself that was an artist in order to do so. As a result of her desire for achievement, she stopped her fine-art work. She is a very talented artist and rediscovered her art early in her recovery, which led to a lot of satisfaction. Her artwork is part of her spiritual life and is therefore basic to her healing and recovery at that deep personal level. Instead of verbalizing the message or handling it in a direct way, her messages were acted out through the cocaine use. In early recovery, it is important for patients to get in touch with the message or messages they are not usually aware they are sending.

When she came to understand the messages she was sending, Marium made some radical changes in her life. The first was to leave her lover, who was not meeting her needs, and the second was to return to her artwork, which was deeply satisfying. The third was to get back in touch with her family and with the Judaism that had always been an important factor in her life, and which she ignored during her heavy cocaine use. As she made these changes, her need for a high decreased and cocaine became less a part of her thoughts and desires.

Like all other cocaine addicts, Marium discovered that she could not go back to using cocaine socially after being addicted to it. As I said in chapter 1, it is impossible to go back to social or recreational use once you have been addicted to a drug, and this is one of the biggest issues that people need to deal with in early recovery. Because cocaine affects the reward centers in the brain, people have a tendency to remember the highs and forget the lows of cocaine addiction. We have a long memory for this type of brain stimulation. It is important to have faith in the recovery process and to realize that these urges and thoughts about cocaine will decrease over time.

Another thing Marium learned early in recovery was that she could get important support from women that she was less likely to get, to the same degree, from men. This kind of support is part of the bonding process that women have with each other, in friendship and also in treatment situations. This is a very powerful force. Part of the treatment process I use involves women spending some time with other women as a source of emotional support for each other.

Another factor in early recovery is diet and nutrition, especially for women. Marium, like a lot of other women I have treated, found that cocaine enabled her to lose weight and maintain the loss. As a very fashion-conscious individual, Marium liked this part of cocaine use. The weight loss became a cue for cocaine use, and the cue was so strong that if she gained a pound or two she would go back and use more cocaine to reduce. Of course, as Dr. Gold points out (p. 18), using cocaine to control a weight problem is "like using an earthmover to dig a hole for a daffodil bulb." But many an overweight woman can get hooked on cocaine because of the weight loss and the euphoria that make her feel so good about herself, never realizing that the addiction is far more serious than the extra pounds.

It is important for these women to learn the value of regular diet and exercise to maintain a stable weight. Any therapy program working with women and cocaine use must take this issue seriously, for once a woman uses cocaine as an aid in dieting, it will be difficult for her to avoid the drug, especially as she begins to eat again and puts on some weight.

Another task for women in recovering from cocaine addiction often is to reassess their own values with regard to intimate relationships. Many women feel badly in early recovery about some of the things they did sexually. They feel dishonest. They feel they were involved in behavior that was dehumanizing to them. Because so many women begin to use cocaine as part of a sexual relationship, and because many of them have traded sex for cocaine at one time or another, this issue has to be faced. Such women need to understand that they must forgive themselves for the past and go on. Whether or not a woman has been a "coke whore," if in her own eyes she has behaved contrary to her own deepest self-image, she will feel a lot of pain over this issue. This is another time when the woman must put away the whip. We can't correct our past acts and choices, we can only focus on the present. For this reason, assertiveness training is often a helpful tool in early recovery. This is true for both men and women, but women often need to be more assertive, especially in making decisions about sex. They need to learn not to be doormats. Many of the women I have treated in recovery from cocaine addiction were sexually abused or molested as children, and many re-created those abusive relationships with men later on in their lives. To learn new roles and assertive skills to deal with men, these women may benefit from specialized treatment for people who have been sexually molested. There are many helpful treatment programs, such as Parents United, programs that offer a helpful support system and access to treatment for those who have this history.

Many of these issues involve low self-esteem that has become even lower with the drug problem, so anything that builds self-esteem is helpful in recovery. Appearance is very important, and part of the early recovery time is often spent becoming more healthily concerned with appearance. Besides the weight question, some women have to deal with capillary systems around the nose and eyes that break down, giving the appearance of little pimples. A dermatologist can often be helpful here. It is a part of healthy caring about yourself to have such things corrected.

Women in early recovery also often need to see a gynecologist, especially if their weight loss has been severe enough to interfere with their menstrual cycle. With abstinence from cocaine and some weight gain, the menstrual cycle usually returns, but it is a good idea to consult a gynecologist to make sure there are no other difficulties resulting from nutritional deficiencies and general abuse. Such conditions as venereal disease and urinary tract infections are often present as a result of sexual contacts, a general rundown condition, and exposure to bacteria.

We noted earlier that there has been very little research on cocaine and pregnancy, but this is not the time to try to have a child. For the woman who already has children, this is also a very difficult time. A study by Eldred and Washington in 1975 of women's drug abuse noted the extreme difficulties of women who were trying to get off of a drug while also attempting to support themselves and their children. Dr. Loretta Finnegan comments that "the parent role requires a considerable investment of psychic energy plus the practical component of actual time and energy in child care responsibilities at a time when the woman's own self-development may require maximum concentration." If this is your situation, try to understand that time spent rebuilding your life now will pay dividends in a better future for your children. Make the best arrangements that you can and go ahead with what you need to do.

Many women in early recovery also go through a brief period of obsession with sex or a romantic fantasy about a particular person. It is helpful to know that this may happen, because it will help you to avoid embarrassing situations. Some of this material comes up in dreams in early recovery, which are interesting in and of themselves. People often have cocaine-related dreams, panic attacks, or night terrors. This is all part of the recovery process. The unconscious mind also needs to heal. It just takes time. Your unconscious has a "mind of its own," so be patient with it and give yourself a break. Any temporary romantic or sexual fantasies or obsessions will pass in time.

Another issue for women in early recovery is that of safety. Sometimes a woman has needed to consult a lawyer or the district attorney to get restraining orders to keep an ex-boyfriend, dealer, or others involved in old cocaine-related activities away from her. Take good care of yourself in this regard. Protect yourself by changing your phone number or even moving, if that's what you need to do. The local women's shelter or women's crisis support service has had experience with these situations, so call your crisis hotline for information. You deserve to take the best possible care of yourself. It is reasonable to keep people away who would sabotage your efforts.

Treatment programs for women have up to this time usually been geared either to welfare women or to those rich enough to pay for private care. More government-funded centers that specialize in cocaine treatment for women are needed, because in reality women still earn only about 60 percent of what men do, and many of them cannot afford therapy because of the cost. This keeps women from receiving treatment, because women often receive their cocaine from men cash-free, in exchange for sexual favors. When the need for treatment comes around, these women cannot come up with the money to pay for it. And, as I noted, women who are responsible for children may also find that the problems involved in arranging care for their children seem insurmountable, especially because public knowledge of their cocaine use might cost them the custody of those children.

Most treatment programs assume that if the program works for a man, it will work for a woman, without being realistic about the different needs and feelings of women. I will discuss this more in the chapter on treatment resources, but when you look for help with your addiction, bring up the issues that are important to you, as a woman, and make sure the source you are considering is aware of these issues.

11

Men
and Cocaine

Just as there are some unique considerations with regard to women and cocaine, there are also special considerations about men.

I talked in the last chapter about the messages women give with their cocaine use. Men also are acting out feelings by using drugs rather than stating those feelings or taking a direct approach in dealing with them. With men, one of the frequent messages of cocaine use is "I need more freedom." This was the case for John. He had to learn to assert himself in early treatment and say no in situations where he felt that his need for personal autonomy and freedom was being violated. He also needed to learn new patterns to replace the workaholism he had learned from his father, who was also in the construction and general contracting business. John watched his alcoholic father develop a compulsive work habit as a way of not dealing with an unhappy marriage and the personal feelings that he felt at a loss or incompetent to deal with. So John also buried himself in his work and left no time for a life of his own, spending what free time he had with either his wife of his children.

John had no close male friends. This is a problem many men in our society face, because they are not encouraged to bond with other men. Men need to spend time with other men, just as women need other women, and activities that draw them together are very important. John took up fishing in early recovery and began to go away occasionally on fishing trips with the guys. At first Doris did not understand this and showed some resistance. She used her lack of trust in his ability to stay clean and sober as a way of dealing with her fear of his spending time on his own. In other words, she indicated that she was afraid he was going to use cocaine when he went out of town with the guys, although he chose a group who were not users. Fishing for him was a low-risk activity, but part of Doris's anxiety was that she was not used to John spending time away from her and being a person on his own. This is quite common in marriages, even though it is unhealthy for a couple to rely on each other for all their support. They need a circle of friends and they need to socialize in mixed-sex situations, but they also need to socialize in same-sex situations. So all-male groups are an important part of early recovery.

Men need freedom, time with other men, and acceptance from the women in their lives. In short, they need space, and they need women who support their having this kind of autonomy. Doris had to learn, in early recovery, to trust John to take care of his personal needs, some of which had nothing to do with her but involved relationships with other people.

Another need that men have in early recovery is to recognize a wish for excitement and stimulation. Many men want to have some risk and challenge in their lives, and often their cocaine use pattern reflects this. John, for instance, needed to have some high-risk sports activities in his life to meet his needs for challenge. He took up parasailing and windsurfing, partly to get away on his own but partly because of this need for challenge. He, like many other men—and women—liked to push limits, so he chose activities which have danger attached to them to provide some risk in his life. These sports meet the need for challenge in a way that does not involve drugs, and in fact they would be highly self-destructive and dangerous if done under the influence of drugs. John knew this, and he had a conscious desire to stay alive and get his thrills through high-adventure sports.

It is important to recognize the need in early recovery for physical and mood stability as described in the "Recommendations" section of chapter 4. This is particularly important for men because they often have an uneven physical and mood pattern as part of their working day; they feel up for part of the day and down for the rest. During the down portion the urge for cocaine can set in, in order to restore the energy level and sense of excitement.

Men especially need to be aware of proper diet in maintaining a stable blood sugar level and mood during their day. They need to take their vitamins and eat a proper diet as part of their recovery program, and people like John, who are workaholics, need consciously to schedule breaks for meals and get some relaxation. This is critical to recovery, because otherwise you are setting yourself up for urges for cocaine.

It is important for the wives of men who are recovering from cocaine addiction to realize that they must take that leap of faith and trust their husbands again. Men who want to please the women they care about, and keep them happy, will respond to this kind of trust in a very strong way. If they are trusted, they will do everything they can to be trustworthy and responsible husbands and fathers again.

A man who has children often becomes, during his heavy usage period, not only an absent husband but an absent parent as well. It is important to reestablish the parental role, and part of the family's recovery is to learn to trust again that this man will make good, responsible decisions about his children. Many men discover in early recovery that they have never appreciated their role as parents the way they do now, and they may spend more time with their children, which is particularly important for sons. Young boys need their fathers as competent and caring role models, and daughters need to learn that men can be strong and vulnerable, so that their future relationships will not carry on the addict's-child syndrome.

I emphasize to people in early recovery that it is important to wait at least sixty days before making major decisions in their lives, such as buying or selling a house, changing jobs, marrying, or divorcing. Not only are their lives usually already in a big mess, their perception has been altered by cocaine use. As I said in chapter 2, cocaine has a profound effect on judgment, and it takes sixty days or more to be really clean, not only physically but mentally. Waiting will help assure that they make solid decisions that they can feel good about. Many men want to make career-related decisions in early recovery, sometimes to avoid working in an environment where they know cocaine is available. Sometimes this is necessary, and sometimes not. Making decisions about separations or divorces is not wise either during this time, as too many of those decisions will be based on guilt over behavior involved in getting cocaine or with other women. Decisions made on the basis of guilt are usually regretted later on.

Often during early recovery couples get in touch with the knowledge that they really do love each other, and this is a time when they are able to rediscover their shared love. Early recovery is a rocky time, and it is important for couples to have faith in each other. Usually their old feelings of caring for each other will surface again as a result of abstinence from cocaine use.

Men in early recovery need to feel that it is okay to talk about their feelings and their fears. They need to know that they are human, and it is okay to cry, it is okay to feel scared, and it is okay to be vulnerable in front of their wives, children, or lovers. During this period some men are able to open up to their feelings for the first time in their lives, and while this may be something their wives or lovers have been asking for in a relationship, when they actually get it they are often afraid. The woman is afraid because all of a sudden this man who has been in the role of the strong one is now vulnerable and human, and the woman feels shaky and childlike. Scary as it is, being a part of a man's discovery of his internal emotional and spiritual world is an exciting adventure for a family or a couple, and this is one of recovery's greatest gifts.

Often workaholic men like John are able to discover that they do not have to live as their fathers lived. Instead, they can develop patterns of relaxing and taking care of themselves, of being vulnerable and feeling human beings, that their fathers were unable to experience in their lives. This is another gift of recovery.

Many men also have sexual insecurities and fears in early recovery, but most of these can be corrected by acknowledgment and education. In early cocaine use there tends to be a lot of sexual interest and activity, but with progressive use, as I have said, there is deterioration in sexual functioning. A man may experience periods of impotence at this time, and this can be very frightening. Another gift of recovery is that men discover that they are not sexual machines, whose purpose is to put on a performance, but vulnerable human beings for whom sex is part of a whole experience of relationship, involving feelings as well as the physical act. A man whose experiences have indicated that he is only attractive, or more attractive, if he has cocaine available will also have to work through this insecurity when he again begins to look for a relationship.

Men also may have a tendency toward pain and inflammation in joint areas, and some men may feel that they have early signs of arthritis or bursitis. This should always be checked by a physician, but often these apparent inflammations are the result of cocaine use, and with abstinence the inflammation decreases and then goes away. Because of this, men find that they are able to be more athletic in and after early recovery, and this builds self-esteem. They may either gain back weight that they lost or lose weight gained as a result of heavy drinking during cocaine use. Another gift of early recovery is that many men end up in better physical shape than they were before as a result of learning about proper diet, nutritional supplementation, physical workouts, and body-building activities.

And men may also discover their spirituality. Sometimes this is through meditation or relaxation activities learned in treatment, but whatever the method, they gain a sense of peace that counteracts the restlessness so many men assume is a necessary part of life. They learn to be real men, not copies of media stereotypes, and this is perhaps the greatest gift of all.

12

Cocaine Use
in
the Electronics Industry

My main emphasis so far has been on cocaine use and its effects at individual, couple, and family levels. However, I would not want to neglect mentioning the fact that cocaine use in industry has a profound effect, not only on the individuals who use it but on other people as well, and potentially in terms of public safety risks. A number of firms in the electronics industry have federal contracts that require people to work with sensitive information and designs for new products. Some firms are involved in designing products that may end up being used in transportation. In both cases, there is a large potential risk to the public if these products turn out to be defective in some way.

For example, let's say that a man involved in quality control for an electronics company has a serious problem with cocaine that affects his judgment and perception, as we have discussed. This person will *feel* perfectly able to do his job, although this may not be the case. But because judgment and perception are both affected, products that are defective or questionable may get through a quality control check, when otherwise they would have been rejected. Let's say we are talking about a small part that will eventually end up in an airplane engine. It is the job of the quality control inspector to pick up on defects, especially repeated defects in the same part, and reject those parts requiring further work or a new design. If this person does not do the job, a defective part or a series of parts that are defective might escape detection, be produced, and eventually end up as part of a mechanical or electrical component. I think the potential risk here is quite obvious and needs to be addressed.

I'd like to share a few statistics concerning the electronics industry in California's Silicon Valley that I've collected. I have seen 440 patients who were employed at engineering-related Silicon Valley industries. Of the 440, 25 percent work in quality control. Because so many work in this area, I was interested in potential problems of public safety and national security, so I asked these people to make an estimate of the percentage of cocaine-dependent people who were working side by side with them at these companies. These estimates ranged from 40 to 70 percent. That is to say, 40 to 70 percent of people at small to major-size companies were cocaine dependent! That's quite a statistic. But I find it believable when I think of the number of people that I have seen personally and the reports that I have heard over the years.

I feel additional concern that the executives of these firms, by and large, do not realize the scope of the problem. Many of them are aware that cocaine use is a problem with regard to lower-level personnel: engineering technicians and production workers. However, they are not aware either of the extent of the problem throughout the company or of the extent of the problem with regard to key employees—quality control people, design engineers, supervisory and managerial engineers—people I see all the time.

I have also heard estimates of the financial loss resulting from cocaine use in industry. One medium-sized company (with 600 employees) lost $2 million in 1984. Discussions with management made it clear to me that they attributed much of this loss to cocaine use by their employees.

In the beginning, the person who tries out cocaine

while working at a job that carries with it a lot of pressure seems to produce more. However, as time goes on, the same individual not only produces less but continues to think that he or she is producing more, because perception and judgment change as a result of cocaine use. And so this same individual works on and on and on, very much like a person on a treadmill, never really getting anywhere but believing that miles and miles have been covered. Because cocaine use gives the illusion of competence and productivity, the use and the lack of effectiveness both continue. The financial situation at many of these companies is now beginning to become apparent to the executives, and steps are being taken to deal with the problem. However, in some cases, they are not always the most effective steps to take initially. That is to say, increasing security and bringing in police and dogs perhaps have a certain place in dealing with this kind of problem. However, people are much more likely to step forward and admit that they have a problem if they know they will receive support and referrals for treatment. Many are valuable employees and would be even more valuable if they were drug-free. Estimates made over the past few years of the increase in effectiveness of employees after treatment for drug abuse range from 40 to 50 percent. This in itself would seem to be an incentive to send people to treatment rather than put the money into search-and-arrest operations with dogs and covert spies, as is happening in a number of companies.

It is unfortunate that there have been a number of suicides in some of these companies and a number of overdoses which are cocaine related. Even this is not always enough to wake up the top brass and cause action to be taken with regard to these problems. These executives should learn to recognize the signs of cocaine use and abuse and to make referrals for treatment without penalizing the employee. It has been shown time and time again in the alcohol treatment field that this approach

is more effective, particularly when a problem is just beginning to manifest itself.

Certainly, cocaine use on the wide scale it has reached
today affects a number of industries, but I have chosen
to concentrate on the electronics industry here because
the effects are so dramatic. Lawyers and doctors and
nurses have problems with cocaine as well, and the potential hazard there is also quite profound.

Because cocaine affects perception to the degree that
the user feels okay when this is really not the case, it is
particularly dangerous for physicians and nurses. In some
cases a physician or a nurse may feel okay to go in and
work with patients because the cocaine provides a sense
of confidence. However, in reality, the performance is not
up to usual standards. This is true for lawyers as well. It
is even true, as we saw for Josh, that lawyers presenting
a case in front of a jury will use cocaine. There is a gap
between a person's perception of his or her performance
and other people's perception of it. That is why it is so
important to confront cocaine users and let them know
what their actual performance is, because they really do
not know themselves. It takes several months of abstinence from cocaine for judgment and perception to return
to the pre-cocaine level.

More and more, people who have had problems with
cocaine are coming out and offering help to others. This
is especially significant in the professions. Lawyers and
doctors in particular are much more likely to respond
favorably to other lawyers and doctors in treatment. They
open up to a much greater degree with members of their
own professions who have recovered. This is true for
engineers as well, and a lot of peer counseling could be
effectively carried on within the electronics industry. This
is beginning at a couple of firms, but it needs to happen
throughout the industry.

The first step is to admit that there is a problem. This
is often the largest and most challenging step of all. The

second step is to develop a policy, from top management down, that covers recognition of the problem and referral for treatment. This second step involves training managers and supervisory personnel to recognize cocaine use and abuse in their colleagues, make an appropriate referral for treatment, and support the person who needs treatment. The third step involves monitoring that person's work performance and providing some peer counseling and support at work, even after treatment has occurred. It is also important to set a positive example for employees by staying straight on the job yourself if you are a supervisor or a manager. A manager or supervisor is a powerful role model, and any manager who goes into treatment and gets help affects all employees in a positive way.

13

Gifts in Recovery

It comes as a surprise to many of my patients that drug addiction and recovery are gifts, like packages wrapped in shiny paper and left under the Christmas tree. We can choose to ignore these gifts and leave them under the tree or we can unwrap them and take a look inside. If we unwrap them, we often find that there are tremendous benefits there for us. Most of my patients feel so negative and depressed when they first come in for treatment that they don't understand why they should even bother going through the efforts of quitting the drug. There are lots of payoffs.

The gifts of early recovery are gifts that most people were not open to receive earlier in their lives. They can make many discoveries about themselves as human beings on all four planes—physical, mental, emotional, and spiritual—that they might never have made without cocaine as a stimulus. Here are some examples.

Mental gifts. Patients report a sense of clarity, a new sense of purpose and direction in life, the ability to concentrate and read a complete book or passage, the ability to remember information, and the ability to be increasingly productive in their work. Josh, for example, experienced so much increased effectiveness in his law practice that he doubled his income. Part of this was because he was thinking very clearly, once he was clean and sober, his decision-making was very good, and his work was more effective. When I told Josh I was writing this book, he said that the biggest mental gift he received was clear perception in thinking. From the age of 13, when he started using drugs, he felt that there was a fog or haze between him and the world. He didn't feel that anymore, and it was a great relief.

Emotional gifts. When I mentioned to Marium that I was writing this book and was going to talk about some of the emotional gifts in early recovery, Marium said that her greatest gift was that she could now be really honest with herself about what she wanted in her life and in her relationships with others. She became involved in a relationship with a man who treated her very well, and this was the first time in her life that she had known this kind of love. Marium said she had never been open to being treated well before because she didn't feel she deserved it and didn't know how to receive it. The ability to be in touch with our feelings and to be able to express them rather than acting them out in self-destructive ways is a very great gift.

Physical gifts. Some of the physical gifts involve a sense of strength and competency in people's relationships with their bodies, often for the first time in their lives. For others, it is a return to a time when they felt very healthy and experienced a sense of physical well-being. Sometimes these people have been run down physically for so many years that they have forgotten what optimum health is, if they ever knew it. It is a great gift just to be alive when we look at the statistics on deaths from brain hemorrhage, stroke, cardiac arrest,and respiratory arrest as a result of cocaine use. An old Irish expression is appropriate here: "He has an angel on his shoulder." My patients often tell me that they believe someone was watching over them and protecting them. People who have experienced the ravages of addiction can be grateful just because they are still alive.

Spiritual gifts. Often the biggest spiritual gift in recovery from cocaine addiction is simply to know that there *is* a spiritual side to existence. Many people who develop a problem with cocaine have never really given themselves time to discover the spiritual aspects of life, whatever that means to them. They never allowed themselves to know that there is a greater purpose in life beyond individual daily existence. For some people, recovery from cocaine addiction is a rediscovery of their spiritual desires and goals; for others it is a time when they learn new ways to express the spiritual side of their lives. This is important for a sense of balance in life—a sense of perspective beyond immediate needs and desires. With it comes a sense of peace and serenity.

Other patients offer these new experiences or understandings that they have gained in recovery:

My husband hasn't hit me since I have been clean.
I'm spending more time with my son.
I want to get up in the morning and go to work.
I'm able to eat now.
I have my health back.
I have my health for the first time in my life.
I don't have fainting spells anymore.
I don't use as easily anymore.
I'm looking good physically.
I have increased self-esteem.
I'm able to communicate with my husband.
We go out now as a family.
I read more, and my concentration is a lot better.
My memory has returned.
I have a more positive outlook on life.
I don't have those crusty rings around my nose anymore.
I can read the paper through now and my concentration is better.
I can think clearly now.
I'm able to leave town now without feeling paranoid about leaving my dealer.
My self-esteem was so high in coming off the cocaine that I felt able to get braces for the first time in my life.
I'm more focused on the present.

My income is higher and my investments are better.
I can be around people and feel comfortable doing so.
I'm able to give and receive love.
I have a more positive view about relationships with the
    opposite sex.
Sex is much better.
I trust myself and my own intuition more.
I'm much more assertive.
I'm in sync with time now; I have a realistic perception of
    time.

You can give yourself some of these gifts by starting on your own recovery. And the best time to begin is right now.

14

Treatment Resources

This book is not intended as a directory of treatment resources for help with cocaine addiction in the United States, but I want to mention a few points relevant to these resources.

The first point involves choosing a treatment provider. Please do not assume that all health care providers—for example, psychiatrists, psychologists, social workers, and counselors of various types—have training in substance abuse treatment or further training in the cocaine addiction treatment specialty. Always ask your helper what his or her training has been with regard to substance abuse and, more specifically, cocaine addiction. Most counselors and therapists do not include substance-abuse counseling training as part of their educational program, although some have sought out that training on their own later on. Please bear this in mind and ask about background. You have a right to know what experience your counselor has, and what specialized training is available through the treatment facility you have chosen. Some facilities specialize in alcohol treatment, and others have taken a broader approach and include other drugs. Because cocaine use is so compelling and because many cocaine abusers also abuse other drugs, you need to know whether the resource you are considering can help with your particular problem.

There are national resources you can call to help you find the best treatment resource in your area. The most comprehensive is the Cocaine Hotline, a free confidential telephone referral service operating out of Fair Oaks Hospital in Summit, New Jersey. The phone number is 800-COCAINE; and there is someone there to answer your call 24 hours a day. This service has enabled many people to find help, and I recommend it highly. They provide referrals nationwide, so no matter where you live they will know of a treatment resource close to you. Although they are the most comprehensive, there are other hotlines and referral services available as well.

Another point to consider is that it is important to receive the right level of treatment. There are several choices for treatment: as an outpatient, as a patient in the hospital, as a residential inpatient, and for the long term. All are important and helpful in various stages of the disease. For instance, outpatient treatment is most helpful for those who are not sure how serious their situation is and want an evaluation in the referral. In this case it is appropriate to set up an outpatient evaluation session with a therapist who knows substance abuse to receive recommendations about the kinds of treatment available. Outpatient treatment as a complete treatment form is most helpful for people who have a lot of other resources working for them in their lives, people whose families are still intact, who are holding a job, who have a source of income.

Those who have begun to lose their resources tend to do better in inpatient treatment because their disease has progressed to a more serious level. They are more likely to experience success by changing their environment, and going into a hospital or residential treatment setting helps to break the pattern of use. They need to develop new support systems, because quitting the drug itself is only 40 percent of the problem. The other 60 percent is developing a new life-style to support staying clean, and this often means making radical changes. People who are injecting or freebasing cocaine are usually at a stage where they can quit only if they change their environment. Because residential and hospital treatment are much more successful at this stage, I would recommend strongly that basers and shooters consider inpatient or residential treatment right away.

Outpatient treatment can act as a bridge for individuals who are not ready to acknowledge the need for hospitalization or a residential program. The therapist can work with them over several sessions to help them realize the seriousness of their condition and make a wise choice regarding the most appropriate treatment option.

Although there are many treatment resources, I am mentioning only a few because they are facilities where the staff is particularly sensitive to treatment of cocaine addiction and the personnel are trained in this specialty.

I can't emphasize the importance of the Twelve Step program too much. Not only Alcoholics Anonymous but Cocaine Anonymous, Narcotics Anonymous, and Overeaters Anonymous and their allied support groups use this valuable program. The central office of Alcoholics Anonymous in your community can supply schedules of meetings of these programs, and the central office of Cocaine Anonymous in Los Angeles will supply a listing of meetings around the country if you call (see p. 67). In order to stay clean, people need to make many changes in their lives, and the Twelve Step programs afford the opportunity to work on the kinds of changes that are essential for people who are addicted to cocaine or other substances. Please also remember that people who are addicted to one substance are at a higher risk for addiction to others, and people who have problems with cocaine very often already have problems with other substances as well. Alcohol in particular can be a serious problem along with cocaine, and the alcohol problem needs to be treated at the same time. Because of this, the cocaine addict needs to learn how to use a program that can help maintain a clean and sober life-style.

For families, I strongly suggest Al-Anon and similar programs for the family and friends of the addicted individual. As I pointed out earlier, the recovering addict may also find some of these programs valuable if he or she is dealing with a partner who is addicted or has a history of alcoholism or other addiction in the family. You can also get in touch with these groups through your local office of Alcoholics Anonymous. Addiction is truly a family illness, and for recovery to proceed, the whole family must be involved in the treatment effort. They need to recover with the addict. They, too, can benefit from the gifts of recovery.

Conclusion

We have covered a lot of ground in this book on quitting cocaine. I have intentionally omitted a lot of technical and statistical information, not only because it wouldn't be helpful but also because we still have much to learn about the drug and about addiction. Researchers disagree on almost every point, and those who use the drug, whether recreationally or addictively, often have yet another opinion.

The important thing to know is that for some people, at least, cocaine is highly and dangerously addicting. These are perhaps a small percentage of the population, but it is very difficult to know in advance whether or not you are one of them. If you are, even trying cocaine once is once too often. It seems that people who become addicted to cocaine may often have had difficulties with another drug, or with alcohol or work or food, but this is not always true. We can draw up a composite picture of a sample of addicted men and women, as Dr. Gold and his Cocaine Hotline have done, but even with this in front of us we can make no predictions about any individual.

Not only is it difficult to get definite "facts" about cocaine, even if we had them we would have difficulty getting them out to the general population. The image of cocaine in the media is seductive and attractive, and present and future users are so disinterested in hearing the negative side of this glamorous drug that our message would go against not only what Americans have heard about it but also what they want to hear. Lee I. Dogoloff, Executive Director of the American Council on Marijuana, comments in a 1983 lecture that "not only will the prevention message have to counter those well-established images, but it will have to convince Americans that some sources of pleasure are dangerous." The members of the drug society of the '80s are not long-haired hippies, they are apparently successful people who seem to have earned the right to their fun.

It is just this acceptance that makes getting off cocaine and staying off so difficult. Unless you choose your company very carefully, cocaine is likely to turn up at almost any party or be offered to you by a colleague or be a part of the next sexual relationship you build. Because of this, you must, if you are quitting cocaine, work within the structure of a program and understand that the quitting will affect as many areas of your life as the cocaine did: physical, mental, emotional, and spiritual. Quitting will make a difference, for better or for worse, in all your relationships; it will change your self-image and your public image; it will, in short, require that you rebuild your whole life. Thousands of people all over the United States are taking on this challenge right now.

I can only say that if you are one of the new members of this very courageous club, you will need all the help you can get. I hope you find the treatment program that is right for you, and that you and those who care about you can work together to put the lives damaged by your cocaine abuse back together. There's an angel on your shoulder, too, who has kept you around for another chance. Helping hands are there for you, so reach out and take one. And welcome back!

Bibliography

There are a number of more or less scholarly works on cocaine, but I am discussing the more popular books in this bibliography. An excellent overview is Dr. Mark S. Gold's *800-COCAINE* (Bantam Books, 1984), a resource book that includes information gained from over 500 interviews done by the Hotline staff with cocaine abusers.

Another excellent resource is Michael Weiner's *Getting Off Cocaine,* which is subtitled *"Thirty Days to Freedom: The Step-by-Step Program of Nutrition and Exercise"* (Avon Books, 1984). Dr. Weiner emphasizes a practical method of returning to good health after quitting cocaine, and I have followed some of his suggestions in my recommendations.

How to Get Off Drugs, by the Editors of *Rolling Stone,* written by Ira Mothner and Alan Weitz (Rolling Stone Press/Simon & Schuster, 1984) is another practical source of information, billed as "everything you should know to help someone you love get off—and stay off—drugs, including when to seek help and where to find it."

An older, more popular book on cocaine is Richard Ashley's *Cocaine: Its History, Uses and Effects* (St. Martin's Press, 1975; soft cover ed., Warner Books, 1976). Ashley is something of an apologist for cocaine use and firmly states his opinion that many if not most of the negative side-effects of cocaine are not found in real life. Unfortunately, my patients have told me otherwise.

Cocaine: Seduction and Solution by Nannette Stone, Marlene Fromme, and Daniel Kagan (Clarkson N. Potter/ Crown Publishers, 1984) does describe the negative side-effects in detail.

For those who prefer a more scholarly approach, Robert C. Peterson and others' *Cocaine: A Second Look,* edited by David E. Smith and Lee Dogoloff and published in 1983 by the American Council for Drug Education, offers several short chapters on cocaine's history and current use.

And there is Ronald K. Siegel's "Monograph on Cocaine Smoking," which was an entire issue of the *Journal of Psychoactive Drugs,* October-December, 1982. Dr. Siegel gives an even more complete review, which focuses on the relatively new habit of smoking cocaine after preparing a freebase mixture.

Finally, the National Institute on Drug Abuse, at 5600 Fishers Lane, Rockville, MD 20857, can supply other information and publications on cocaine abuse.